UNDERSTANDING ME

Reproducible Masters for Building Life Skills and Self-Esteem in Teens

**Dianne Schilling
Gerry Dunne**

Editor: Dianne Schilling

Copyright © 1992, Revised 2010, INNERCHOICE PUBLSHING • All rights reserved

ISBN – 10: 1-56499-0070-9
ISBN – 13: 978-1-56499-070-9

INNERCHOICE Publishing
15079 Oak Chase Court
Wellington, FL 33414

www.InnerchoicePublishing.com

The purchase of this book entitles the buyer to reproduce pages as needed for classroom use only. All other reproduction for any purpose whatsoever is explicitly prohibited without written permission. Requests for permission may be directed to INNERCHOICE PUBLISHING.

UNDERSTANDING ME

**Reproducible Masters
for Building Life Skills and Self-Esteem
in Teens**

Contents

Introduction 7

Feelings, Thoughts, and Behaviors 13
Feelings Are ... .15
Being a Teenager 17
Self-Esteem 19
What's Important to You? 21
Culturally Speaking, You're Special 23
Learning to Learn 25
You Are Creative! 27
Communication 29
Tell It Like It Is 21
The Art of Listening 33
Friendship 35
Belonging 37
Discovering the Real You 39
Heroes, Models, and Villains 41
Leadership 43
Following the Leader 45
Winning and Losing 47
Brains, Courage, and Heart 49
Handicaps and Limitations 51
Decisions, Decisions 53
Decision Making 55
Know Where You're Going 57
The Informed Decision 59
Decisions & Consequences 61
Critical Decisions 63
Solving Problems 65
Know Your Goals 67
Control Your Time 69
Take Charge! 71

Assertiveness	**73**
Influence	**75**
Pressure!	**77**
Responsibility	**79**
Earning, Spending, and Saving	**81**
Get a Job!	**83**
The Way I See It	**85**
To Trust or Not to Trust	**87**
Helping	**89**
Managing Conflict	**91**
How to Resolve a Conflict	**93**
What is Justice?	**95**
Tales of Justice	**97**
Showing Initiative	**99**

Introduction

UNDERSTANDING ME is a collection of reproducible activity sheets designed to help middle-school and high-school students develop important life skills while enhancing their self-esteem and self-awareness.

When students feel competent to deal with life's many challenges, they feel good about themselves, and when they feel good about themselves they are capable of higher performance and achievement in all areas.

The self-esteem of students can so profoundly influence whether or not they reach academic goals that improving their estimations of themselves and their capabilities deserves to be a goal in itself—one that guides academic and interpersonal interactions with students on a day-to-day basis.

As educators, we know that the way to reach a goal is to establish specific, relevant objectives, and to plan and carry out the steps required to meet them. *The goal of high self-esteem in students is no exception.* Our conduct as educators ought to be characterized by behaviors that demonstrate our recognition of the worth and worthiness of *all* students at all times. Rapport and respect should be established whether we are counseling, engaged in after-school instruction, or teaching English, math, science, or physical education. It takes a lot of work and dedication to manage a group of teens in a fashion which guarantees that every student feels valued, develops an awareness of his or her capabilities, and regularly experiences success. But the effort greatly enhances the student's ability to learn, and is repaid to us over and over again.

The social and emotional learning of students is enhanced by the development and acknowledgment of identifiable life skills.

Schools frequently overlook these critical skills because they are *non-academic*. Yet all students, whether gifted, talented, average, or slow, require them. Research demonstrates that when deficiencies in the development of life skills exist, students are "at risk." On the other hand, as life skills are acquired, performance goes up and self-esteem is enhanced. This holds

---

Self-esteem is the sum of all that a student has come to believe about him or herself in a qualitative sense. It is the student's unique perception of his or her worth and worthiness.

true for all socioeconomic levels, all cultures, and for every other environmental condition or circumstance.

In virtually every area of living life skills are needed. Along with math, science, technology, history and English students also need to be taught how to manage themselves, their time and activities. They need to know how to get along with others and to formulate goals and communicate their needs in a pro-social manner. Too often these critical life skills are not addressed in a direct fashion but their acquisition is simply left to chance. Students often don't learn effective ways to deal with life issues. They have ideas but can't express them clearly. They get into conflicts they don't know how to resolve. They have hopes and dreams but can only drift through life. Often it's the lack of skills and awarenesses that prevent many from becoming fully capable, contributing, happy members of society. School is the ideal places to directly teach life skills, both for their impact on the future and because life skills ensure the effective application of academic skills today.

Understanding Me develops, maintains, and enhances critical life skills. Among the life skills addressed in these activity sheets are:

- **decision making**
- **goal setting**
- **communication**
- **conflict management**
- **learning**
- **leadership**
- **time management**
- **responsibility**
- **assertiveness**
- **career choic**
- **trust**
- **friendship**
- **culture**
- **justice**

In addition to your own enabling behaviors and the cultivation of an affirming classroom or counseling environment, you can assure a positive impact on the social-emotional development of your students by infusing these activities into your regular curriculum or counseling efforts. They represent one of many possible approaches and can be enlisted as supplements to other strategies you are currently using.

How to Use the Activity Sheets

Each 2-page sheet contains a separate, independent activity. The sheets may be used in any order, and duplicated in quantities sufficient for distribution to the students in your class or group. Here are some recommendations for their use:

■ **Sequence activities.** While all activity sheets are separate entities and may be used independently, a few series do exist. For maximum impact, distribute sequential activity sheets in the order in which they are arranged in the book. Sequences include:

- **Feelings**
  (2 activities, pages 13-16)
- **Communication**
  (3 activities, pages 29-34)
- **Leadership**
  (2 activities, pages 43-46)
- **Decision Making**
  (6 activities, pages 53-64)
- **Goal Setting**
  (2 activities, pages 67-70)
- **Influence**
  (2 activities, pages 75-78)
- **Conflict Management**
  (2 activities, pages 91-94)
- **Justice**
  (2 activities, pages 95-98)

■ **Use regularly.** Life skills deserve regular attention. Try to distribute at least one activity sheet a week. Allow students 20 to 30 minutes to complete each sheet.

■ **Relate to academic assignments or to current community or school events.** Topics like trust, friendship, communication, justice, culture, etc., are so thoroughly woven into the fabric of everyday life, you should be able to relate them fairly easily to what is happening in class or group, both academically and interpersonally. Such connections will enrich your subject or topic and add immediacy to the activities themselves.

In order to accomplish anything worthwhile in life and realize our full potential we have to develop some meaningful life skills.

- **Encourage interaction.** Everyone working with teens knows that socializing is one of the primary preoccupations of teenagers. Developing positive peer-group relations is also one of the developmental tasks of adolescence, so why resist? After students have completed their activity sheets, ask them to get together in two's, three's, or small groups and discuss what they have learned. Some activity sheets specifically suggest such interaction.

- **Generate group discussions.** After giving students a few minutes to complete an activity sheet privately, use some of the questions or topics from the sheet as discussion starters.

- **Respect privacy.** Never *require* that students share what they have written. Although the activity sheets do not probe sensitive areas, students will occasionally write something that they prefer to keep confidential.

- **Create spin-off assignments.** If several students show particular interest in a topic area, create a research team to unearth more information and report back to the class. Or suggest that the group use the information to create a new activity sheet for students to complete.

- **Develop presentations.** Use the information contained in an activity sheet as the basis for a presentation or group activity that you develop.

- **Use the skills.** Watch for opportunities to reinforce life skills by practicing them in the context of real-life situations. For example, have students set academic goals for your class, using the information on page 67. When you observe a student trying to make a decision, have the student follow the decision-making process outlined on page 55. If a conflict erupts, refer students to the conflict management strategies on page 93.

The competencies students gain from the use of these activity sheets in conjunction with related classroom or group counseling experiences will contribute to a reservoir of skills from which they may draw strength for many years to come. We hope that *your* role in building that reservoir will be enjoyable and rewarding.

Feelings, Thoughts, and Behavior

As human beings, we *feel*, we *think*, **and we** *behave*. Thoughts, feelings, and behavior relate very closely to one another and are virtually impossible to separate. Thoughts trigger feelings, and feelings in turn motivate us to act. And that's just one possible sequence. We're lucky we've got all three ways of experiencing. They fit together perfectly!

Feelings

Whether or not you understand your feelings, they are always there. Some emotions are **enjoyable**, and others are **miserable**. Occasionally, we have feelings that we can't even describe. And sometimes, we feel good and bad about the same thing. **We** *feel* **our emotions in our body**.

What feelings are you having right now?

_____
_____
_____

Where and how (in your body) do you feel those emotions?

_____
_____
_____
_____

Feelings happen inside of you, but very often, they show—in your **facial expression**, **tone of voice**, and **posture**. People who look closely can sometimes *read* your feelings. They can see if you are smiling or not, whether your eyes are sparkling or worried, and whether your walk is heavy or light. The way you *behave* tells people how you are feeling.

In general, how are people "reading" you today?

- **Facial expression**
  ___relaxed
  ___worried
  ___bored or tired
  ___angry
  ___happy

- **Tone of voice**
  ___pleasant
  ___harsh
  ___weak

- **Posture**
  ___erect, but relaxed
  ___closed, stiff, or tight
  ___dragging, slumped
  ___tense or combative

Your feelings don't *always* show. Sometimes you hide them. The reason might be to keep from hurting someone else, or to protect yourself.

Can you think of a time recently when you hid your feelings? How did you do it?

_____
_____
_____

Why did you do it?

_____
_____
_____

Occasionally, people are so confused by their feelings that they try to shut them off. They won't let themselves experience feelings, and they don't like other people to show their feelings, either. Unfortunately, when you shut yourself down to protect yourself from having *unpleasant* emotions, you run the risk of turning off the *pleasant* ones, too.

Thoughts

You are a thinking creature. Some of the ways you think are very obvious. You think when you figure out a math problem or a riddle, when you plan a trip or party, or when you decide how to handle a problem or difficult situation.
Describe a problem (big or small) that you've solved today:

_____
_____
_____
_____

Sometimes you have *fantasies*. You might sit and daydream and imagine all kinds of things and not know how active your mind has been. Or an idea might pop into your head that doesn't feel comfortable. So you make it disappear and forget it ever happened.

You **calculate**, **make judgments**, **plan**, **believe**, **fantasize**, **solve problems**, **decide**, and **wish**. Sometimes you are aware of your thinking processes, and sometimes you aren't. When you think, the thoughts themselves don't show unless you turn them into behavior.

Because you can share your thoughts out loud by speaking with someone else, you can do things that no other form of life on our planet has been able to do. **Your ability to think puts you in charge of your own life**.

Try this…

Begin a private journal by writing down at the end of each day:
1. At least two things you did that you are pleased about and one thing that you wish you had done differently.
2. Some of your most important thoughts.
3. Something that you are looking forward to.

Behavior

You are constantly behaving, and **your behavior shows**. Right now, you are reading this. Perhaps someone is near you who does not appear to be doing anything. *Look again.* The person is engaged in sitting, standing, looking, fidgeting, or some other form of behavior.

Your behavior is often the product of your feelings and thoughts. The more you are aware of your feelings and in control of your thoughts, the better able you are to take charge of your actions.

Which — feelings or thoughts — is probably governing behavior in these statements:
"He acted irrationally."
"She made a careful decision."
"He was moved by their story."

Below, write down 4 things that you like to do. For each thing, write down some of the feelings you have as you do it, how long it has been since you did it, whether it is something you do alone or with at least one other person, and how much it costs.

1. Activity: _____
   Feelings: _____
   Last did this: _____
   Do alone? _____ With others? _____ Cost: _____

2. Activity: _____
   Feelings: _____
   Last did this: _____
   Do alone? _____ With others? _____ Cost: _____

3. Activity: _____
   Feelings: _____
   Last did this: _____
   Do alone? _____ With others? _____ Cost: _____

4. Activity: _____
   Feelings: _____
   Last did this: _____
   Do alone? _____ With others? _____ Cost: _____

What did you learn about yourself from this exercise?

Feelings Are...

...Universal

How many feelings are there? Nobody knows for sure. But we do know that everybody feels them all. In that way, we're all alike. However, what triggers the feelings varies from one person to another, and so does and the manner in which they're expressed. In that way, each of us is unique.

Have you ever noticed how differently two or more people can react to the same event? When Corky, Shirley's puppy, chewed up her new shoes, Shirley was **furious**. Her mother was **irked**, her father was **disgusted**, and her brother was **amused**. He thought it was funny.

Think of a time when something like this happened to you. Talk about it with a classmate.

...Confusing

Feelings can be strange and confusing. The word *feel* itself can cause confusion. We use it not just to express emotions, but to voice thoughts, and to describe sensations. We say "I feel we should call him." when we mean "I *think* we should call him." We say, "I feel too hot," referring to the physical sensation of heat. We say, "This surface feels rough," describing something we've touched. Can you distinguish the difference? **Read the following statements. Put a "T" beside those that represent thoughts, an "S" beside those that describe sensations, and an "F" beside those that express emotions or feelings.**

____He feels tired.

____I feel we can do it.

____She feels scared.

____We feel hungry.

____He feels lonely.

____I feel cold.

____I feel this is important.

____He feels inspired.

____We felt disgusted.

____My head aches.

____She feels we're making a mistake.

____The boy felt miserable.

____My toe hurts!

____He felt that a change was needed.

____I felt humiliated.

____She anxiously waited for the bus.

...Ambivalent

Have you ever noticed how often feelings come in pairs or threesomes? We frequently experience more than one feeling at a time, and sometimes our feelings do not agree. Frequently, we experience positive and negative feelings about the same thing. We're *ambivalent*.

The root word *ambi* means "movement." And movement is exactly what occurs. Our attention moves back and forth between one feeling and another. The result is conflict—a sort of fight between the feelings inside us.

Can you remember having mixed feelings when you:

1. had your hair cut?
   Feelings: _____

2. came home from a trip?
   Feelings: _____

3. let someone borrow something?
   Feelings: _____

4. were given a big responsibility?
   Feelings: _____

5. played a trick on someone?
   Feelings: _____

...Transparent

No matter how much people try to hide their feelings, most of the time their feelings show. If you collided with someone in the hall and didn't want the person to know you were hurt, you could say, "It's okay, don't worry about it." But if you were holding your side and your smile looked like a grimace, do you think the person would believe you? Your body language—facial expression, posture, tone of voice, etc.—often speaks louder than your words.

What feelings can lead to these body reactions?

Tears _____

Smile _____

Lump in throat _____

Pounding heart _____

Sweaty palms _____

Clenched fists _____

Shaky arms, legs _____

Bouncy walk _____

Red face _____

Tight stomach _____

Frown _____

Trembling jaw _____

Slouched posture _____

...Functional

Our feelings help us function in thousands of ways. For example, have you ever become frightened and, because of your fear, done something to protect yourself from a real danger? It makes sense to be scared of certain things. People lock doors because they fear burglary or other intrusions, and they wear jackets in icy weather because they fear frostbite.

Below is a list of feeling words. Pick one or two, and see if you can briefly explain the use of that emotion in human life. Tell how you think it works for you.

anger	indecisiveness
pain	joy
satisfaction	hope
power	love
courage	patience
fatigue	silliness
eagerness	protectiveness
curiosity	anxiety

_____

_____

_____

_____

_____

_____

_____

Being a Teenager

Have you ever thought to yourself, "Nobody understands me?" Why? Do people expect more of you now? Do they want you to take on new responsibilities? Are you getting new privileges or permission to do things you couldn't do before? Do you have some new problems? Or do you sometimes feel like a child one minute and an adult the next? Maybe it seems that when it comes to privileges, adults still see you as a child. But when it comes to responsibility, they see you as an adult.

Teenage years are filled with changes!

Some of the most dramatic changes are **physical changes**. Your body is changing from a child's body to an adult's body. Other changes are **mental**—you're getting smarter! And still others are **emotional**.

What are some of the changes that you are aware of that are happening now in your life? Here's a chance for you to write down how you feel about each one. Remember, feelings can be pleasant or unpleasant, but they aren't good or bad, right or wrong. Feelings simply are.

The Changes	Your Feelings
New responsibilities:	
New privileges or ways to enjoy yourself:	
New problems:	
New physical changes:	

What's Your Opinion?

What do you enjoy most about being a teenager?

1. _____
2. _____
3. _____
4. _____
5. _____
6. _____
7. _____

What do you dislike most?

1. _____
2. _____
3. _____
4. _____
5. _____
6. _____
7. _____

What special things are going on in your life right now that you always want to keep as a part of you?

_____
_____
_____
_____
_____
_____

What problems or difficulties are you facing now that you do not want to carry into adulthood?

_____
_____
_____
_____
_____

Will these problems resolve themselves as you grow and mature?
____ Yes. ____ No.
If no, what can you do about them?

_____
_____
_____
_____
_____

If you decide to become a parent or a teacher, what will you try to remember about teenagers when you live with or teach them someday?

_____
_____
_____
_____
_____
_____

Self-Esteem

Mirror, Mirror, in My Mind

You've probably heard the terms *self-image* and *self-esteem*. Do you know what they mean?

Self-image is the *picture* you have of yourself. Self-esteem is how you *feel* about that picture. If you like the picture (the total person, not a photograph or image in the mirror), if it makes you feel strong, powerful, and capable, then you probably have high self-esteem. If you don't like the picture, if it makes you feel inferior, powerless, and incapable of doing things well, then you may have low self-esteem. Of course, your self-esteem can be anywhere in the middle, too. And it can change!

Here's a way to clarify your picture of yourself. Put a single check (√) next to the words that describe the way you are now. Put a double check (√√) next to words that describe qualities you haven't expressed yet but feel will emerge as you develop and grow. If you don't know what some of the words mean, see if you can find out.

___active	___cheerful	___generous	___inventive	___optimistic	___tolerant
___adventurous	___clever	___good-natured	___likeable	___organized	___tough
___affectionate	___competitive	___honest	___logical	___patient	___trustworthy
___aggressive	___cooperative	___humorous	___loyal	___reliable	___understanding
___ambitious	___determined	___idealistic	___methodical	___responsible	___uninhibited
___artistic	___discreet	___imaginative	___musical	___sensitive	___verbal
___attractive	___efficient	___independent	___natural	___spontaneous	___versatile
___businesslike	___emotional	___individualistic	___open-minded	___strong	___warm
___calm	___flexible	___intelligent	___opportunistic	___tactful	___witty

Getting to Know You

Complete these sentences to get better acquainted with the unique person who is you:

I am a person who _____

_____

Something I wish others knew about me is _____

_____

One of the things I feel proud of is _____

_____

One of the nicest things I could say about myself right now is _____

_____

The best thing about being a child was _____

_____

The thing I most need to improve in myself is _____

_____

Controlling Self-Talk

When you were very young one of the main ways you developed self-esteem was by paying attention to how your family, teachers, and friends treated you, and how they talked about you. If they liked you and thought you were a worthwhile person, then you had good reason to feel the same way about yourself. Today, what others think of you is still important, but even more important is what you think of yourself, and what you *say* to yourself. Now that you are no longer a child, the most powerful influence on your self-esteem is your own **self-talk. Here's how self-talk works:**

You do poorly on a math test, so you say to yourself:
Negative: "I'll never get this. The teacher is just a big jerk anyway. I'm so stupid.
Positive: Obviously there are some things I'm not getting, but I'm sure I can do better. I think I'll ask for some extra help.

Try It!

1. You are told to clean up your room. You say to yourself:
Negative: "I'm such a mess. I can't do anything right. I just can't get organized.
Positive: _____

_____

2. Your best friend invites someone else to go to the movies.
Negative: He/she probably doesn't like me anymore. I'm no fun to be with anyway. I'm a bore.
Positive: _____

_____

3. When called upon to give an oral report in class, you become so flustered that you forget everything. Afterwards you say to yourself:
Negative: I made a fool of myself. I can't face those guys. I'll have to cut class tomorrow.
Positive: _____

_____

4. You ask someone you really like to go to the school dance. He or she says no, without giving a reason.
Negative: I'm not good looking (fun, smart, etc.) enough to ever be popular. No one wants to go out with me.
Positive: _____

_____

What's Important to You?

Have you ever noticed how people value things differently? Knowing our likes and dislikes, and what is *valuable* to us, helps us make good decisions about how to act and what to choose.

Here are two stories about situations that have something in common. See if you can explain what it is.

1 For months, Shirley has been looking forward to going with Harold to the most important dance of the year. Harold has been looking forward to it, too. But the day before the dance, Shirley's uncle and aunt come to town with her cousins, Tom and Elena. Shirley enjoys being with her cousins and her aunt and uncle so much that she doesn't know what to do when they invite her to go on a 4-day boating trip with them. They plan to leave immediately and, if she goes, Shirley will miss the dance.

If you were Shirley, would you go on the boating trip, or would you go to the dance with Harold? Give your reasons.

_____

How do you think Harold would feel? _____

_____

Have you ever been in a spot like this? **Write about it and tell how it caused you to feel:**

_____
_____
_____
_____
_____

2 Don is upset. His older brother, Kyle, has allowed Bill (Kyle's friend) to ride Don's bike. Kyle and Bill don't seem to feel very guilty about it because Don wasn't using the bike at the time. In fact, Bill says that he thinks Don is being stupid to get so annoyed. This really upsets Don—so much that he yells at both Kyle and Bill, saying that they can forget his promise to let them play with his pinball machine. At this point, Kyle socks Don as hard as he can.

Who behaved worst in this situation? Next to worst? Least badly?

Don _____

Kyle _____

Bill _____

Why? _____

What Do You Want?

What we want often changes as we grow older. Sometimes we want two or more *conflicting* things. **In the end, how we act and what we choose are the most accurate indications of what is important to us.**

Do you know what you want? Write down the three things you want most in your life:

1. _____

2. _____

3. _____

Now, write down an **action** you have taken lately that is related to each thing you listed:

1. _____

2. _____

3. _____

What Would You Do If . . . ?

1

You have been told that you have only six months to live. Fortunately you will remain healthy until the week before you die. A generous but unknown benefactor has heard of your plight and has offered you the following gifts:

1. You may visit any six countries in the world and spend as much of the six months in each country as you wish.

2. You may use any means of travel you wish, and you have unlimited travel within and between the six countries.

3. You will receive $5000 a week for expenses.

4. You may take one other person with you.

Will you go?

_____ Yes _____ No

Why or why not? _____

_____

_____

_____

If you go...

Which countries will you visit and for how long?

1. _____

2. _____

3. _____

4. _____

5. _____

6. _____

How will you travel?

_____

_____

In what places will you stay?

_____

_____

What will you do?

_____

_____

What will you buy?

_____

_____

Whom will you take with you?

_____

2

Your house has caught fire, and after calling the fire department you realize that everything may be destroyed. You figure you have enough time to make three trips from the house, carrying whatever you can carry in your arms. No one else is in the house, including pets. What would you take out?

First Trip:

Second Trip:

Third Trip:

Culturally Speaking, You're Special!

What's one difference between human beings and all other animals?

Human beings are creatures with cultures.

Your culture may determine:

—the **language** you speak.

—your **religion**.

—the **music** you're used to hearing.

—the **dances** you've learned.

—the **food** you eat.

—the way you **dress**.

—the way you spend your time and money.

—your notion of good and bad, right and wrong.

—the **customs, holidays,** and **ceremonies** your family observes.

—the kinds of relationships you have with other people.

—the things that are important to you.

You may belong to more than one cultural group. Many people do. Our country is a big mosaic of cultures.

Other things influence you, too. Where you live, how much money you have, and whether you are male or female, for instance. *But the culture you've been born into has a lot to do with who you are.* Your friends too are who they are partly because of their cultures.

Most of the time people don't think about being part of a culture until they are in a new place. Have you ever gone to a strange place and suddenly felt uncomfortable? When this happens it's called culture shock. *Can you remember a time when you experienced culture shock? Describe what happened here:*

_____
_____
_____
_____
_____

How would you answer this question: *What is the name of your culture?*

_____
_____

People in various groups often look at people in other groups as "different." Some of these groups have to do with **sex, age, physical size, education, religion, race,** and **ethnicity**.

In our country, some people assume that the White (Caucasian) culture (which is really a collection of cultures) is better than other cultures. They think this partly because more people belong to it.

It's important to remember that *most* does not always mean *best*. This kind of unaware thinking has led to a lot of problems between people of different cultures. Many individuals miss out on enjoying other people and other ways of experiencing life because they make negative judgments about other groups. The White American culture is *one* way to be, but it is not *the* way to be. **Your cultural differences make you special, unique, and interesting!**

Look at Your Roots

Fill in as many names as you know in the blanks on the family tree. If you were adopted, it doesn't matter. Just fill in the names of your adopted family. *Culture is something we learn, we aren't born with it.*

Next look at each name on the tree, and think about who each of these people is or was *culturally*. You are the product of these combined cultural influences.

Talk to your parents about the culture of your family. Ask them if there are any cultural practices they did with their families when they were your age that your family doesn't do now. Find out as much as you can about how and why things have changed.

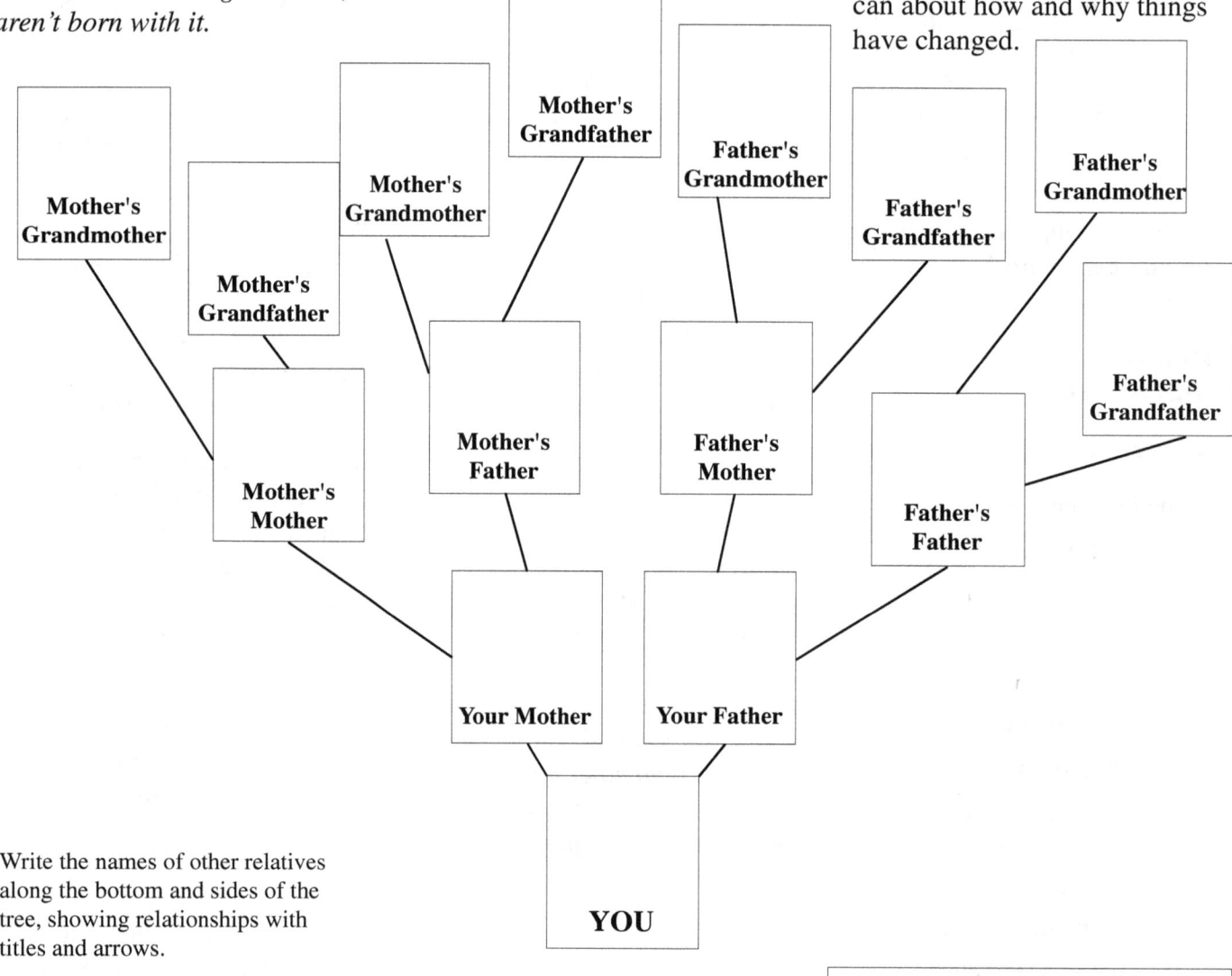

Write the names of other relatives along the bottom and sides of the tree, showing relationships with titles and arrows.

Give—and Take—Cultural Credit

See how many things you can list that you like about yourself that are part of you because of your culture.

1. _____
2. _____
3. _____
4. _____
5. _____
6. _____
7. _____
8. _____

What are some of the things you appreciate or enjoy about a friend whose culture is different from yours?

1. _____
2. _____
3. _____
4. _____

Learning To Learn

I GOT THIS LITTLE WHITE RAT AND I BUILT A MAZE TO SEE HOW QUICKLY IT COULD LEARN TO FIND ITS WAY THRU...

I WOULD CHANGE THE MAZE EVERY 3 TIMES... THAT RAT GOT SO CONFUSED... BUT HE WOULD LEARN TO FIND HIS WAY THRU THE MAZE... THEN I'D CHANGE IT...

NOW... WHICH WAY DID THAT RAT GO...? LEFT... RIGHT... NO... LEFT...?

Look at All You've Learned!

What is learning? To learn is to gain knowledge, understanding, or skill through study, instruction, or experience. Learning is something we do all the time, whether in school or out. The human brain is a learning machine that keeps on running for as long as we live.

As a baby, you were 100% involved in the process of learning. You learned by touching, exploring, tasting, watching, and listening, to name just a few methods. You loved it then. Do you still like to learn?

Have you noticed that when you are *truly* interested in a subject or activity, learning is effortless? You absorb knowledge like a sponge and perfect skills so rapidly that when you look back, you can't even remember how it happened!

It's hard for many people to admit how much they've learned. Being honest with ourselves is sometimes very difficult. For example, can you look at the past and the present and really pinpoint where your successes have been?

Use the unfinished sentences and questions on this page and the next to get you started. Think about the things that you have learned to understand. Think about the skills that you have acquired. Think too about the inner qualities that you have developed.

Questions

- How did you learn to ride a bicycle? _____
_____
_____
_____
_____

- How did you learn to play monopoly or your favorite electronic game?
_____
_____
_____
_____
_____
_____
_____

More questions ⟶

- What are five things you've learned quickly and easily? (school subjects or anything else)

  1. _____
  2. _____
  3. _____
  4. _____
  5. _____

- What are some things you've been able to show other people how to do?

  1. _____
  2. _____
  3. _____
  4. _____

- What are your major talents and capabilities?

  1. _____
  2. _____
  3. _____
  4. _____

- What are some of your major accomplishments?

  1. _____
  2. _____
  3. _____
  4. _____

Discover the Process

Is it possible to learn everything?

Of course not. But remember that learning is not just a set of facts, it's a process. **The most important part of learning is to learn *how to learn*.** Parts of the process are *discovery, wondering, observing, experiencing, trying, experimenting, doubting, sharing, comparing, questioning, evaluating,* and *creating.*

Think of something you *enjoyed* learning. Not after you were finished, but *while* you were learning it. Consider the process that you went through. Try to remember how your mind approached the task and what made it enjoyable? **Talk it over with a friend.** Then answer this question:

I can make learning more enjoyable all the time by. . .

The Tough Stuff

Everybody has trouble learning some things. You aren't alone. Here are some things kids your age say they have trouble with sometimes. If any of these apply to you, just put a check mark next to the item:

__1. Using my time well.

__2. Standing up for myself when I know I am right.

__3. Keeping up my self-confidence.

__4. Giving myself credit for my past achievements.

__5. Giving myself credit for my strengths.

__6. Admitting my mistakes.

__7. Learning from my mistakes.

__8. Having a conversation with a stranger.

__9. Speaking in front of a group.

__10. A particular school subject. (What?)

__11. Solving problems.

__12. _____

Think over each item you checked. Set a goal to overcome the one or two weaknesses that bother you most. Make a step-by-step plan for reaching each goal and then start putting those plans into action. If you don't know how to go about it, ask someone to help you. **When you reach a goal, reward yourself!**

You Are Creative!

- Phil creates the lyrics for songs.
- Lisa creates the music.
- Manuel draws and paints fantastic pictures.
- Heidi and Keith created a robot that they control with their computer.
- Larry creates winning football plays.
- Irv creates prize-winning short stories.
- Dana creates great hamburgers.

HEY! LOOK, WE'VE GOT THIS GREAT IDEA!

People can be creative in the ways they use words, numbers, music, and art. They can be creative in sports, science, writing, student government, and cooking. And they can create in lots of other ways, too. **So can you!**

Exercise Your Creativity!

Can you remember things you created as a child? Maybe you made up a game, or created a fort or hideout, made someone a present, or put your own ending on a song or story. See how many things like this you can list:

1. _____
2. _____
3. _____
4. _____
5. _____
6. _____
7. _____
8. _____
9. _____

The creative child inside you is not lost. Since creativity is a way of looking at the world, you can allow the child in you to express him or herself whenever you want.

Use as many of these words as you can in a paragraph or short story. Write your story on another sheet of paper. The sillier you can make it, the better.

kangaroo	volcano
mud	boy
garage	fake
snooping	leaping
cloud	paper clip
horrid	moon
petunia	glass
terrific	cautiously
midnight	raced
girl	box
amazing	sorry

Complete the sentences below. Use your imagination. Be serious, funny or artistic.

In the pit of his stomach, Josè felt _____

_____

_____

As she called out to me, I knew _____

_____

Poor guy. He didn't realize yet that _____

_____

What's in a Name?

Print your first name in the space below. Then add lines and forms to each letter. Make them become animals, faces, plants, machines, or interesting designs.

Creative Connections

Connect the dots with lines in any way you wish. Add more dots and lines, fill in spaces and use colors if you like.

Recycling Fun

In two minutes, list as many ways as you can think of to use an old refrigerator. Do this with a friend.

What keeps you from being creative? Is it embarrassment, being afraid you won't be best, or fear of criticism? List some of your creative blocks here:

1. _____
2. _____
3. _____
4. _____
5. _____

What stimulates your creativity? Music? Creative people? Alone time? Describe some of the those things too:

1. _____
   _____
2. _____
   _____
3. _____
   _____
4. _____
   _____

Pay attention to your ideas. When you get an idea, no matter how silly it seems, give it your attention. Don't dismiss it from your mind. Think it over for a while. If nothing develops right away, turn it over to your *unconscious* mind. A few hours or days later it may return—in a form you can really use.

Communication

Breaking the Code

In order for two or more people to enjoy and encourage each other, to work, play, or solve problems together, they need to be able to communicate effectively.

In every example of communication, no matter how small, a message is sent from one person (the sender) to the other person (the receiver). The message tells the receiver something about the feelings and/or thoughts of the sender. Because the sender cannot "give" the receiver his or her feelings and thoughts, they have to be *encoded* in words. Good communicators pick words that describe their feelings and thoughts as closely as possible. Nonverbal "signals" almost always accompany the verbal message; for example, a smile, a frown, or a hand gesture. Sometimes the entire message is nonverbal. Good communicators send nonverbal signals that exactly match their feelings and thoughts.

When the receiver hears (and sees) the coded message of the sender, he or she must *decode* **it.** This means that the receiver must not only understand the meaning of each word, but must interpret the meaning of the entire message, including nonverbal signals. **Study the diagram.**

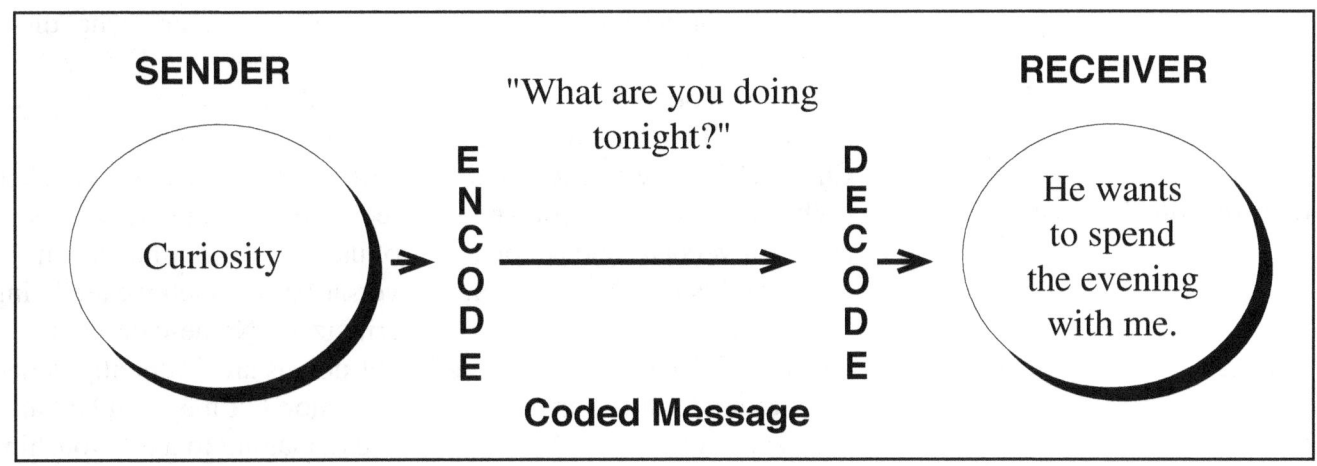

29

Slip-ups

You can probably see why there are so many slip-ups in communication. Many times a sender just *assumes* that the receiver knows what he or she means. Other times, a receiver thinks "Oh, I get it." and completely misinterprets the message.

Describe a recent incident in which your communication was misinterpreted.

_____

_____

_____

*Why do you think this happened?*_____

_____

_____

_____

Describe a recent incident in which YOU misinterpreted the communication of someone.

_____

_____

_____

How did this happen?_____

_____

_____

_____

Communication Blocks

Here are more behaviors that can seriously hamper communication—or stop it altogether.

Interrupting/Dominating
People interrupt because they:
1. get impatient when a speaker is slow to transform a thought into a statement (encode a message).
2. are reminded of something they want to say and can't wait their turn.
3. are more interested in their own thoughts and ideas that in those of others.

Have you ever tried to have a conversation with a person who continually interrupts you? How do you feel when this happens?

Advising
"Well, if I were you..." or "I think you should..." or "Take my advice and..." By giving unasked for advice, a person immediately takes a position of superiority. Advice-giving says, "I know better than you do."

Judging
Not only does a "judge" assume a superior position in conversation, his or her judgments may be completely wrong. For example, suppose you say to someone, "I have a dog named Charlie." The person responds, "What a good person you are—all dog lovers are fine people. What kind is it?" You answer, "A poodle." Your listener responds, "Oh, that's too bad. Poodles are high strung and hard to train."

Probing
Asking lots of questions tends to put the speaker on the defensive. More importantly, questions can lead the speaker away from what he or she wants to say. For example, suppose you are trying to describe your day to a friend. But as soon as you mention the first thing that happened, your friend asks, "What did you do that for? What happened? What did she say?" etc.

Accusing/Contradicting
Suppose while talking to some friends, you say, "I wrote this paper on my computer." One of the friends jumps in with, "No you didn't, since when have you had a computer?" You respond, "I bought it with money I saved." To which the same friend says, "You never have any money, so how could you save money?" Contradictions and accusations put the speaker on the spot and cause him/her to get defensive.

Criticizing/Name-calling/Putting-down
Suppose you say, "I have a dog named Charlie." Your listener responds, "You jerk, what did you get a dog for? You can't even take care of that mangy cat of yours!"
Criticism can make the speaker feel wrong or unworthy. Few of us want to continue a conversation in which we are being criticized. Name-calling and put-downs are frequently veiled in humor, but may still be hurtful and damaging to a relationship.

Tell It Like It Is

Creating Clear Pictures

When two people have a conversation, they take turns being the sender and the receiver. First one talks while the other listens and then they switch roles. Both the sender and receiver have a responsibility to ensure that understanding takes place.

To send clear messages, remember that the same words don't bring the same picture to everyone's mind. So be as specific as you can about the way you use words.

Try to be sure inside yourself about what you want to say. Ask yourself, "What are my intentions?" When you are clear about the message, everything about you—your words, tone of voice, posture, and facial expression—is consistent.

Ask for feedback. Suppose you have said something to someone and you want to be sure that the person understood your intent.

Here are some things you could say:
"How do you feel about that?"
"What's your reaction to what I just said?"
"I'd like to hear your thoughts."
"What's your understanding of my idea?"

If, upon checking, you realize that your listener failed to understand what you said, *change the code*. Restate your thought in different words. Then ask for feedback again.

Think about a time you were involved in a misunderstanding because someone didn't know what you meant. Write about it here:

What could you have said differently that might have avoided this misunderstanding?

Send an "I" Message

When you are the sender, one of the most powerful messages you can send—especially if you are having a problem or conflict with the receiver—is an "I" message. An "I" message tells the receiver what the problem is, how you feel about it, and what you want (or don't want) the receiver to do. Many times, we send "you" messages when we would be much better off sending "I" messages. "You" messages are often blaming and threatening, frequently make the receiver feel mad or hurt, usually make the situation worse, and many times don't even describe the problem.

Here are some examples of "you" messages:
"You're such a klutz. Can't you do anything right?"
"You're so sloppy. Get these things picked up right now!"
"It's your fault. If you'd done your part, this wouldn't have happened."

Compare them to these "I" messages:
"When I see you carrying the baby like that, it scares me. I'm afraid she might get hurt."
"When your room looks like this, I feel very discouraged. I want it to look nice like the rest of the house."
"When you don't do your part of the assignment, we all suffer. I want to get a good grade, so please finish by tomorrow."

"I" messages are also good for sending positive messages, like compliments, praise, and expressions of love and happiness:
"I like your outfit. I think you look fantastic."
"I feel so good about this. Thank you."
"I'm glad we're friends. I have so much fun with you."

How to Do It

1. **Describe the situation.** It may help to begin with the words, "When..." or "When you..."

2. **Say how you feel.** "When you........................, I feel............ ...."

3. **Describe what you want the person to do.** "When you......................, I feel....................., and I want you to............................"

"**When you** don't pick up your things, **I feel** scared that Mom will ground us both. **I want** you to help keep this room clean."

Practice

Your friend borrows your camera to take to a party at his uncle's house. He forgets to bring the camera home, but tells you not to worry about it—it's in good hands—and promises to pick it up the next day. The next day, he doesn't have time to go by his uncle's house, and the following day he forgets. This goes on for a week, but your friend keeps saying, "Hey, don't worry. I'll take care of it." **You say:**

_____

_____

_____

_____

You and your sister (or brother) are watching T.V. together. You ask to see the T.V. guide, but she doesn't give it to you. She tells you, "There's nothing else good on." Your sister keeps the remote in her lap and won't let you have that either. This happens almost every time you watch T.V. together. **You say:**

_____

_____

_____

_____

The Art of Listening

Hearing the Real Message

When someone is talking to you, your job is to listen. Even more than that, you need to hear, to watch, and to sense. It's an art!

Listening can be difficult, especially when a speaker disguises his or her message. Sometimes people are too embarrassed or afraid to come right out and say what they want to say.

Suppose your friend asks you, "I'd look pretty good if my nose weren't so big, don't you think?" Inside, your friend hopes you will say, "Your nose is just right and you look great!" And if you are able to hear and sense what he or she *truly needs* at that moment, you'll respond to the *real* message.

Do you know someone (a friend or teacher perhaps) who knows how to listen so well that when you say something to him or her, you really feel understood? Does this person sometimes hear you even in silence? What is the secret of people like this? What do they do?

Chances are they look directly at you, and they seem interested in what you're saying. They may ask a question or two for clarification, but they usually don't interrupt much. They may repeat in different words (paraphrase) what they hear you say. Or they may focus on the feelings or meaning behind your words, so you feel heard on a deep level. You may not be aware of it, but they are probably noticing other things too—your nonverbal messages or "body language," which give added clues to the meanings and feelings behind your words.

Think of someone you know who is a good listener. Try to idnetify all the things he or she does that shows good listening.	How do you feel when you are with this person?

How Does It Feel?

Can you remember a time when someone really listened to you? Describe what happened and how you felt about the person.

_____
_____
_____
_____
_____

Can you remember a time when you listened well to someone? How did the person seem to feel about you? _____
_____
_____
_____

How did you feel about yourself? _____
_____
_____

Mastering the Art

- **Listen in order to understand.** Don't get ready for what you are going to say next.

- **Pay attention to more than words.** Notice tone of voice, facial expression, posture, etc.

- **Try to put yourself in the speaker's shoes.** Listen for feelings.

- **Put aside your own opinions for the time being.** You can't listen to your own thoughts and someone else at the same time.

- **Be patient.** Listening is speedier than talking, so don't jump ahead of the speaker.

- **Show your interest and empathy.** This can encourage a speaker to say more, to dig deeper into an issue or problem.

- **Don't interrupt.** Ask questions only when clarification is needed.

- **Clear up misunderstandings before you begin your own talk.**

Beyond Words

Read through this list. These are ways we communicate who we are to other people

*Flashing eyes, wide eyes.
Wrinkled brow.
Curled lips, smiling lips, laughing lips.
Lip biting, teeth grinding.
Quick movements, or slow.
Arms crossed, moving hands, legs crossed, toe twitching.
Slouching, standing tall.
Personal care: teeth, nails, nose, skin, hair.
Clothing: tight, loose, revealing, concealing, fancy, plain, "in," "out-of-style," bright, drab, neat, sloppy.
Your handwriting.
Your closet.
Your wallet.
The books you read.
The way you walk down the hall.
Clear your throat.
Look at people, carry things.
Doodles.
Humming.
Handshake: bone breaker or wet towel?*

Can you think of more? **List other nonverbal ways people communicate here:**

_____
_____
_____
_____
_____
_____

Friendship

What Is a Real Friend?

	AGREE	DISAGREE
1. Someone who knows all about me and likes me just the same.		
2. Someone who always agrees with me.		
3. Someone who doesn't care how much money I have.		
4. Someone who'll do whatever I say.		
5. Someone who listens to me, even if I'm talking about my troubles.		
6. Someone who expects me to see things exactly the way he or she does.		
7. Someone who would try to stop me from doing anything that might be harmful to me.		

If you agreed with numbers 1, 3, 5, and 7, you have probably had some real friends during your life. They knew and liked you in spite of things like whether or not you were broke. They also cared how you felt. They listened to your feelings. That's how they proved they were friends.

If you disagreed with numbers 2, 4, and 6, you realize that everybody is different and that being different is okay. Friends don't have to agree with each other all the time. And they don't always have to do what each other wants to prove their loyalty and friendship.

Friends Past . . .

Examine a friendship of the past. Think of a friend you had when you were a child.

List what you liked about him or her: _____
_____
_____
_____

List what you think he or she liked about you: _____
_____
_____
_____
_____

Briefly tell about one of the best times you ever had together (when, where, what you did, etc.) _____
_____
_____
_____
_____
_____
_____

Present . . .

Examine a present friendship. Think about someone who is a friend of yours now.

How did your friendship begin? _____
_____
_____
_____
_____

List some things you like to do together: _____
_____
_____
_____
_____
_____
_____
_____
_____

What is different about your friendship now and the way it was in the beginning? _____
_____
_____
_____

and Future!

List as many things as you can think of that you want in a friend: _____
_____
_____
_____
_____
_____
_____
_____
_____
_____
_____
_____

If you could take one person with you on a trip around the world, whom would you take? Why?

Name: _____
_____

Reason: _____
_____
_____
_____
_____
_____

Changing and Growing

Just as people change, friendships also change. Sometimes the changes cause friendships to fall apart, and sometimes the changes make friendships better.

Think of a friendship you've had that fell apart. *What were the changes that caused it? Do you have a friendship with someone that almost always seems to be getting better? What have the two of you done to make this happen?*

Belonging

Groups and organizations do not really exist unless they have members. Members "make up" a group, whether the group is a formal one (like an official team) or an informal one (a group of friends). Feelings of being in (included) or out (excluded) occur with both kinds of groups. Think back to some situations you experienced when you were younger. Write down key words that remind you of a situation in one column and your feelings about it in the other, like this:

SITUATION:	HOW YOU FELT ABOUT IT:
A time when you included someone:	
A time when you were included:	
A time when you were left out or excluded:	
A time when you excluded someone:	

If someone wants to join a group that you are a member of now, how do you and the other members decide on whether or not to include him or her?
_____

How do you feel about this way of deciding?
_____

Could it be done more fairly?
___Yes ___No

If yes, how? _____
_____

When do you think it's fair and right to keep someone out of a group? _____
_____
_____
_____

What Works

Think of at least three people whom you **like to have around.** List things you often see them doing when they are with other people:

Person A: _____
_____
_____

Person B: _____
_____
_____

Person C: _____
_____
_____

How would you describe their personalities?

Person A: _____
_____
_____

Person B: _____
_____
_____

Person C: _____
_____
_____

What Doesn't

Now, think of at least three people whom you usually **don't like to have around.** List things you've seen them do when they are with other people (no names, please):

Person A: _____
_____
_____

Person B: _____
_____
_____

Person C: _____
_____
_____

How would you describe their personalities?

Person A: _____
_____
_____

Person B: _____
_____
_____

Person C: _____
_____
_____

Take Inventory!

List **12 of your good qualities**—things you like best about yourself. These are probably the things other people like best about you, too.

1. _____
2. _____
3. _____
4. _____
5. _____
6. _____
7. _____
8. _____
9. _____
10. _____
11. _____
12. _____

Take Action!

All people can improve themselves. *What can you do for yourself that might help you be accepted and included by others more often?*

1. _____
_____
2. _____
_____
3. _____
_____

Decide to be your own best friend. You are unique and special. You deserve your own friendship!

Discovering the Real You

We've all done it. Combed our hair a certain way because we admired the style on someone else. Used a particular verbal expression because our friend used it and we thought it sounded clever. Bought a pair of shoes or adopted a style of dress in order to follow the example of someone we admired.

Think about yourself. See if you can identify some characteristics or traits that you borrowed from someone else—hair or clothing style, political view, way of spending your leisure time, attitude about money, plans for a future career, etc. **List those characteristics on the chart below. Then rate how well each characteristic fits the *real* you.**

A lot of times we adopt a habit, a viewpoint, a way of talking, dressing, or doing things and quickly forget that it didn't start as our own. Sometimes it fits really well with who we are; other times it doesn't.

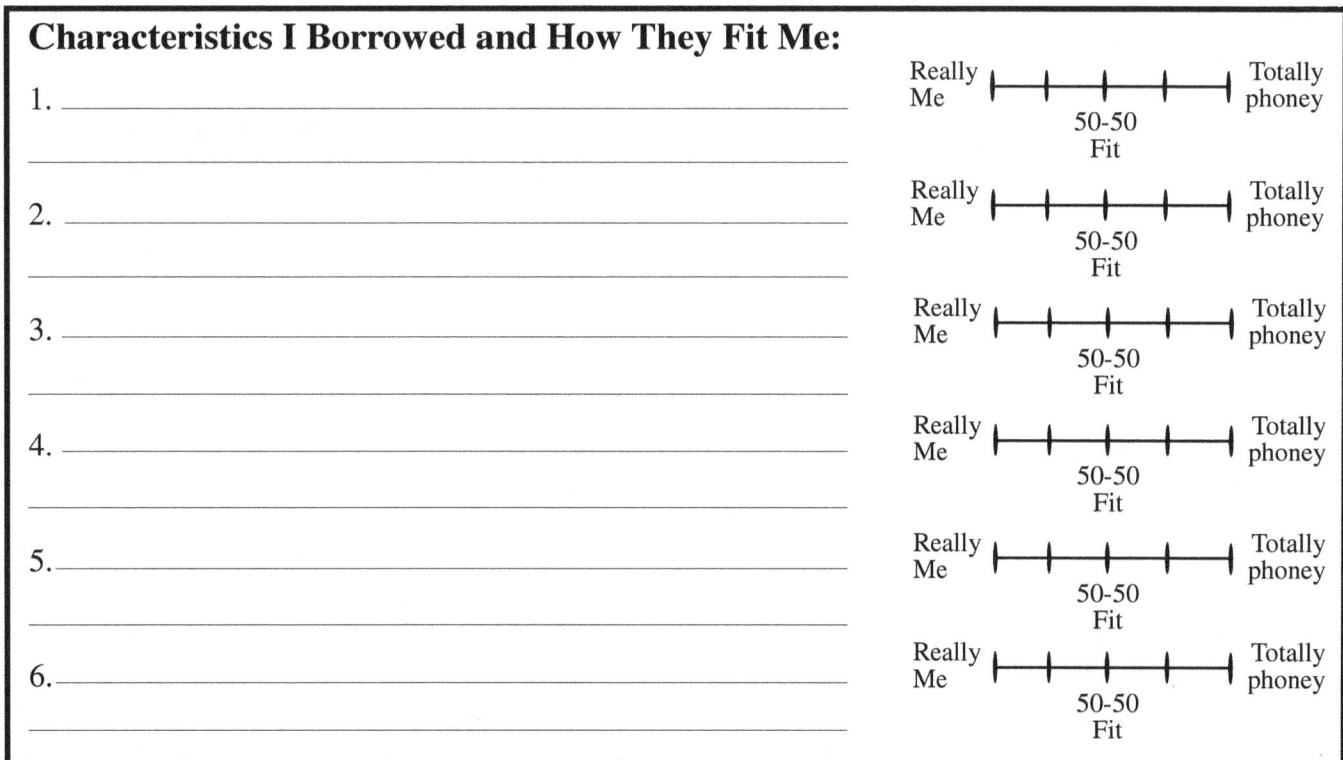

Know Your Own Mind

Why is it that some people are so completely and naturally themselves, while others are always trying to find out who they are?

Self-determination for one thing. Deciding, without doubting, that you are a unique, one-of-a-kind person; deciding that you have your own style and selfhood; deciding that you are *much more* than a collection of other people's opinions, styles, and manners.

Below, list 8 abilities, talents, skills, or personal attributes that make you YOU:

1. _____
2. _____
3. _____
4. _____
5. _____
6. _____
7. _____
8. _____

How many times have you said, " I really should go to the party, because..." and had all sorts of reasons to do it, even if you really didn't want to.

Next time, try saying instead, "I *could* go to the party. But I could also do these other things (identify them). What I really *want* to do is... ."

"Shoulds" and "coulds" come from two different places. Shoulds come from the *outside*. They are often what other people tell us. Coulds come from *inside* us. They are a way of stating possible choices. Doing something because you "should," allows you to avoid accepting responsibility for your action. **Making conscious choices is a way of discovering and developing the REAL you.**

Try This:

Tune in carefully to your thoughts about other people. Notice whether you are being fair or whether you are stereotyping or pre-judging them. Also, notice how you treat others. Are you fair or do you treat them according to false ideas that you have about them?

Take a look around you. Without being a judge, observe other people. See which ones you think are being themselves most of the time, and which ones are trying to be someone else.

Keep a journal. Pick a regular time, such as once a week, and identify something about you that is unique—that you like and feel good about. Describe it in your journal.

Instant Remake

Answer this question: "If I were to be reborn now, how would I like to be different and how would I like to be the same? Use another sheet of paper if you need more space. Share your answer with a friend.

_____
_____
_____
_____
_____
_____
_____

Heroes, Models, and Villains

Heroes

Do you have any heroes? Heroes and heroines are people who do courageous things. Frequently, their actions take great mental, emotional, spiritual, and/or physical strength.

Perhaps your favorite hero is a television or movie character. Maybe your hero or heroine is someone you admire and respect who is a real person. Perhaps you know the person, and perhaps you don't. Heroes can also be people (real or fictional) whom you've read about in books.

Try listing some of your heroes and heroines here:

NAME	REASON YOU ADMIRE
Television hero: _____	_____
Hero in American history: _____	_____
Book hero: _____	_____
Movie hero: _____	_____
Living hero: _____	_____

Suppose for a moment that one of your heroes or heroines could speak to you right now. *What advice would he or she give you?*

_____
_____
_____
_____
_____
_____
_____
_____
_____
_____

Role Models

Have you ever heard the term *role model*? A role model is a person you admire whose behavior serves as a guide for *your* behavior. Since you are a teenager, your role models are probably older teens or young adults.

Can you think of any people who are models for you? Here's a place to list some of them and what they have taught you.

ROLE MODEL	WHAT I LEARNED
1. _____	_____
2. _____	_____
3. _____	_____
4. _____	_____
5. _____	_____

Sometimes people choose other people as role models without realizing they are doing it. For example, a younger student at your school might have picked *you* as a role model. You aren't aware of it, and neither is the younger student. Nevertheless, he or she starts copying your behavior.

Can you see why it's important to know who your role models are? Once you've identified them, you can stop yourself from copying them if they do something that is wrong or harmful.

Villains

How can there be any good guys if we haven't got any bad guys with whom to compare them? For many people, villains are very, very interesting! **Take a minute to list some of your villains.** (They may be real people or fictional characters in books, movies, or T.V. shows.)

1. _____

2. _____

3. _____

4. _____

What fairy tale did you like most as a child? _____

Who was your favorite hero or heroine in the story? _____

What did you like about him or her? _____

Who was the villain in the story? _____

What did you learn from the villain? _____

Leadership

What Is a Leader?

When you were little, did you play "Follow the Leader?"

Most children, when they play this game, want to be the leader. In fact, sometimes children vie with each other for the leadership role. **What about you?** *Did you want to lead or follow?*

_____
_____

What about now? If a chance comes up for you to stand out, take charge, be captain of a team, a committee chairperson, or class officer, do you go for it?

___Yes ___No *Why?*

_____
_____
_____

All of us are leaders at times. Leadership is a *process*, not a person. And in many situations, leadership is shared. Looking at what a leader *does* will help you understand the process of leadership.

A leader *influences* other members of a group. A leader gets the group, or individual members of the group, to do things that move the *whole* group in the direction of a goal. *Have you ever done that?*

Leader Qualities

- **Self-control.** If someone can't control himself or herself, can this person be expected to control other people?

- **A sense of fair play.** When followers are treated fairly, they tend to believe in and respect their leader.

- **Making decisions and plans.** Starting with workable ideas and goals, a leader can make decisions—and stick with them!

- **Taking initiative.** Competent leaders pay attention to details, organize things, and carry through.

- **Being able to get along with others.** Leaders listen to their followers and try to understand what's needed and wanted. They are usually good communicators.

What can you add to this list?

Types of Leadership

Read the situations below. Decide which of these types of leadership is being provided in each one. Circle your answer:
1. Giving directions and information.
2. Offering encouragement and praise.
3. Participating and facilitating (making things easier.)
4. Delegating (turning over a task or project to someone else.)
5. Providing vision and inspiration.

● Manny and Elizabeth are artists for the school newspaper. They are trying to decide how to illustrate the lead story for the upcoming issue. Manny is working on a great computer drawing, but time is getting short and they could use a photo instead. They are having trouble making a decision. Sylvia sits down with them. She listens and asks questions and helps them figure out what to do. **Sylvia is providing leadership by:** 1 2 3 4 5

● Janet is chosen as the understudy for the lead role in the school play. She practices hard and learns the part well. Three days after the show opens, the regular lead comes down with the flu. The drama teacher tells Janet that she will have to perform that night. Janet suddenly becomes frightened and refuses to go on. Jeff, who is also in the play, says to Janet, "Hey you can do it. I've seen you practicing. We really need you tonight." Jeff sticks close to Janet during rehearsals that afternoon and tells her that she's doing a great job. **Jeff is providing leadership by:** 1 2 3 4 5

● While helping each other with their Algebra homework, Chris and Carol start having trouble with a particular type of problem. Carol's older brother, Steve, overhears their struggle and offers to help. He explains how to complete each step of the first few problems and then coaches them as they complete several more on their own. **Steve is providing leadership by:** 1 2 3 4 5

● The student council has decided that the school would benefit from having an official mascot. Some members favor a live pet, and others want a student to dress up and play the role of a cartoon character. Carlos, the student body president, appoints Cindy (an art student) and Tom (a drama student who works part-time at a pet store) to study the issue and make recommendations to the council. **Carlos is providing leadership by:** 1 2 3 4 5

● Eric, a member of the debate team, has been talking to the other members about entering a competition in England. He describes all the fun they'll have and thinks up ways to raise the needed money. Lately, Eric has been distributing passport applications and British tour books. The rest of the team is starting to take the idea seriously. **Eric is providing leadership by:** 1 2 3 4 5

Think of two people you know or have known who were good leaders. Write their names and briefly describe at least one thing each one did as a leader that you felt good about:

Name of Leader: _____

What the Leader Did: _____
_____
_____
_____
_____
_____

Name of Leader: _____

What the Leader Did: _____
_____
_____
_____
_____
_____

Try This

Volunteer to lead. Take a chance at being a team captain, committee chairperson, class representative, tutor, or preschool or elementary school teacher's assistant. Run for office, or become an assistant to the coach of a Little League or soccer team.

Following the Leader

Everyone... ...Gets To Be a Follower

Everyone is both a leader and a follower. Everyone *needs* leadership sometimes, and everyone *gives* leadership at other times. You take the leadership role in one situation, and someone else does in another.

Do you remember the definition of leadership?
Leadership is the process of influencing another person or a group of people to move in the direction of a goal.

Depending on the situation, a leader may:
- give directions and information.
- give encouragement and praise.
- get involved—help solve a problem, lead a brainstorming session, etc.
- delegate a job to someone who is qualified to do it.
- provide vision and inspire others to do their best.

One thing that's apparent is that different leaders (or authority figures) engender different feelings in us. But sometimes people decide (often without realizing it) that *anyone* who is in a position of leadership or authority represents some kind of threat. People who feel this way can make life miserable for the leader, other followers, and themselves.

See if you can think of four times when you've supported a good leader. Name the leaders and then briefly state what you did to let them know you were behind them.

THE LEADER   HOW I SUPPORTED THE LEADER

1. _____ _____

2. _____ _____

3. _____ _____

4. _____ _____

Get the Leadership You Need

One of the places you are most often a follower is in school. In every class, you have a different leader—your teacher. So in every class you are dealing with a different leadership style. Because of this, it's important to identify the kinds of leadership *you need*. What you need will undoubtedly vary from class to class. **Think carefully about each one of your classes. Put a check (√) next to the number that best describes you.**

Subject _____
___1. I don't understand the subject at all. I don't even like to go to class.
___2. I have some trouble with the subject, but I think it's interesting and I enjoy the class.
___3. I can get good grades in the subject, but it doesn't interest me.
___4. I do very well in the subject and I enjoy it, too.

Subject _____
___1. I don't understand the subject at all. I don't even like to go to class.
___2. I have some trouble with the subject, but I think it's interesting and I enjoy the class.
___3. I can get good grades in the subject, but it doesn't interest me.
___4. I do very well in the subject and I enjoy it, too.

Subject _____
___1. I don't understand the subject at all. I don't even like to go to class.
___2. I have some trouble with the subject, but I think it's interesting and I enjoy the class.
___3. I can get good grades in the subject, but it doesn't interest me.
___4. I do very well in the subject and I enjoy it, too.

Subject _____
___1. I don't understand the subject at all. I don't even like to go to class.
___2. I have some trouble with the subject, but I think it's interesting and I enjoy the class.
___3. I can get good grades in the subject, but it doesn't interest me.
___4. I do very well in the subject and I enjoy it, too.

Subject _____
___1. I don't understand the subject at all. I don't even like to go to class.
___2. I have some trouble with the subject, but I think it's interesting and I enjoy the class.
___3. I can get good grades in the subject, but it doesn't interest me.
___4. I do very well in the subject and I enjoy it, too.

Subject _____
___1. I don't understand the subject at all. I don't even like to go to class.
___2. I have some trouble with the subject, but I think it's interesting and I enjoy the class.
___3. I can get good grades in the subject, but it doesn't interest me.
___4. I do very well in the subject and I enjoy it, too.

For each number you checked, read the corresponding paragraph to find out what kind of leadership you need.

1. You need lots of help and supervision. Ask your teacher, parent, a tutor, or another student for step-by-step directions on each assignment. Have your work checked frequently. You benefit most from a teacher who is a "**director**." One who lets you know exactly what is expected of you. You do not have to feel lost and confused. Ask for the help you need. Don't worry about liking the class. As soon as you know what you're doing, you'll begin to enjoy it.

2. You need direction and supervision as you continue to gain skill in the class. Whenever you don't understand a problem or assignment, ask for clarification. You benefit most from a teacher who is a "**motivator**." One who sees that you are catching on, gives you lots of positive reinforcement, and inspires you to try even harder. Get involved in the class. You know enough to ask lots of questions and contribute to discussions. Do it.

3. You are bored with either the subject or the class or both. If you don't need the class, consider substituting one that you like. If the class is required, take responsibility for increasing your levels of participation and enjoyment. Volunteer for an extra-credit assignment that challenges you. Get involved in class discussions. You benefit most from a teacher who is a "**participator**." One who invites lots of class participation and interaction.

4. You are so successful and self-motivated in this class that you don't need much leadership at all. You will do the work whether the teacher is there or not. You benefit most from a teacher who is a "**delegator**." One who trusts you enough to say, "Here's the task—see what you can do with it." This class offers *you* a chance to be a leader. Be creative. Break new ground. Help students who are having trouble with the class.

The teacher is your leader. Ask for what you need!

Winning and Losing

A Look at Competition

Since you live in a competitive society, you are almost always being invited (or pushed) to compete. You compete in sports, with your friends, at school—everywhere. You are graded and given tests. If you want to go to a four-year college, you'll have to compete with other students to get in. When you are an adult, you'll have to compete with other adults to earn a living.

Competition definitely has its advantages. It encourages people to do their best, to develop good products, and to provide needed services. *Can you think of some specific examples that show how competition helps students do better in school?*

1. _____
2. _____
3. _____

Many people dislike a certain kind of competition—the kind that causes people to feel they have to win no matter what, and feel defeated when they lose. *Can you think of some specific examples that show how competition causes students to do worse in school?*

1. _____
2. _____
3. _____

Think of a time when you won at something and loved it. Describe it here:

_____
_____
_____
_____

Describe a time when you lost and felt bad about it:

_____
_____
_____
_____

Have you ever felt excited and challenged by a task because it was a competitive situation? When? _____

_____
_____
_____

Winner or Loser?

When Barbara was 13 years old, she won a spelling bee in her English class. Other classes had spelling bees too, and all the winners from every seventh, eighth, and ninth-grade English class met at a school assembly for a school-wide spelling bee. With everyone in the entire school watching, Barbara won again.

A couple of weeks later, the school district held a run-off for the winners from all the schools, and Barbara won that spelling bee, too. She then became the district's entry in the state contest which was held in a big auditorium at the Capitol. Even the governor was there. And—you guessed it—Barbara won again.

Finally, Barbara went to Washington D.C. for the national contest. The principal of her school, her English teacher, and her family got to go, too. The auditorium was packed with hundreds of people. Television cameras were everywhere. It seemed to Barbara as though everyone in the whole world was watching. She was scared to death. When the contest started, Barbara was the fourth student to go up to the microphone to spell a word. The first three students succeeded. They spelled their words correctly. Then it was Barbara's turn. She had never heard the word before. She thought about it hard and spelled it the best way she could think of, but she was wrong. Barbara was the first person to be eliminated from the contest—and in front of the whole world! It was one of the most painful moments of Barbara's life. For weeks, she felt embarrassed and ashamed.

Which was Barbara, a winner or a loser? Why? _____
_____
_____

Barbara won three times as many contests as she lost, but she still felt like a failure. Why? _____
_____
_____

If you were Barbara's friend, what would you say to her?
_____
_____

Do Your P.B.!

You can compete against yourself to get better at a skill in the least amount of time. This is sometimes called achieving your "personal best." Self-competition can help you improve your performance in athletics, music, languages, dance, and lots of other areas. **Describe a time when you competed against yourself.**

_____
_____
_____
_____

Winners at Life

Everybody loses or fails at times. What matters is the message you send yourself after a loss or failure. Winners are people who aren't afraid to get to know themselves. They like the things that make them different and they like the things that are different and special in others. Winners are responsible. They see themselves as the main person who will make their lives turn out the way they want. Winners are not afraid of their feelings; they are able to give and receive love; they have a zest for life; they care about other people; and they are very happy to be here now. **Everyone can be a winner, including you!**

Brains, Courage, and Heart

Did you ever see the movie, *The Wizard of Oz*— or read the book?

Remember the scarecrow? He thought he was dumb and wanted to get some brains.

How about the lion? He saw himself as a terrible coward, badly in need of courage.

And remember the tin woodsman? He thought he was cold and unfeeling, so he wanted a heart. They went with Dorothy and her dog, Toto, to see Oz, the Great Wizard, to ask him for the things they thought they lacked.

Along the way, whenever they got into a difficult situation, the scarecrow brilliantly figured out how to handle it. The lion bravely risked his life for his companions. And the tin woodsman constantly showed his concern for the feelings of others. Whenever something made him sad, he cried!

When they finally got to see Oz, they discovered that he wasn't a great and terrible wizard after all. He was a phoney. He was a funny little man who pretended to be a ferocious beast.

But they left the palace happy. *Do you remember why?*

Oz gave the scarecrow a degree. The lion received a medal for courage. And the wizard pinned a heart on the tin woodsman.

Somehow Oz was able to convince them that the degree, medal, and heart were *real* and would give them brains, courage and feelings. Sure enough, the scarecrow noticed how bright he had become. The lion felt brave and courageous, and the tin woodsman got in touch with his deep sensitivity and loving nature. **They started to believe in themselves and discovered within them the things they wanted!**

What do you think L. Frank Baum, who created "The Wizard of Oz," was trying to say?

_____
_____
_____
_____
_____
_____
_____

Success Focus

Many people don't know how capable they'd be if they just recognized their abilities and believed in themselves. One reason is that they rarely focus on their abilities:

Here's a chance to focus on some of *your* capabilities. Just complete each of the following sentences:

1. Something successful I did during the first five years of my life was: _____
_____
_____

2. Something difficult that I have mastered is: _____
_____
_____

3. Something I could help a younger student learn is: ___
_____
_____

Take Risks!

Perhaps you are very aware of your weaknesses. Maybe when you make a mistake, it bothers you a lot. You may keep yourself from trying things at times because you want to be perfect.

Lots of people think mostly about their mistakes and weaknesses. They think there are a lot of things they can't do. Even when they are successful, they don't feel good about themselves. Just to make sure they won't fail at something, they use this strategy: *They don't try it at all!* **What's wrong with that strategy?** _____

_____

_____

It helps to remember no one is great at everything. You have your weaknesses, but so does everyone else.

Everybody makes mistakes, too. If you kick yourself after you make a mistake, it probably won't help. What will help is remembering the mistake and not making it again. Stop and think for a moment about a mistake you've made only once (or just a few times). *Not repeating that mistake is a success!*
To avoid criticism:
    do nothing;
    say nothing;
    be nothing.

Believe in Yourself!

Luckily for you, you've already got what the scarecrow, lion, and tin woodsman traveled so far to get.
Use your brains to make things work for you.
Use your heart to give yourself understanding and support.
Use your courage to keep trying!

See and believe in each one of your successes.
Accept failure as the occasional price of trying.

Dream Big!

Think of three of the most wonderful things you could ever do. Pretend that you are actually doing them. Imagine all the details, like who's there and what each person says. **Describe each situation in as much detail as possible, here:**

1. _____

_____

_____

_____

_____

2. _____

_____

_____

_____

_____

3. _____

_____

_____

_____

_____

Disabilities and Limitations

Have you ever thought about how some people's disabilities and difficulties show and other people's don't?

- Bob lost both legs in an automobile accident.
- Eliza has allergies.
- Maria was born blind.
- Omar is tone deaf.
- Shirley is mentally retarded.
- Anna has difficulties with arithmetic.
- Jack has cerebral palsy.
- Jose has kidney failure.

All these young people are students. If you met them, you would see some of their disabilities right away. Others you would not know about unless you were told.

Almost everyone has some kind of disability or difficulty. Maybe yours shows and maybe it doesn't. When a disability shows, it's known as a *visible disability*. **Put a "V" next to the examples of visible disabilities, above.**

A Reality Check

It's important to remember that disabilities are very specific. A person who has a disability most likely has only one.

What would you guess are the real limitations of each of these students?

Eliza: _____

Omar: _____

Shirley: _____

Jose: _____

What are some of the mistakes that people might make in relating to these students?

Bob: _____

Maria: _____

Anna: _____

Jack: _____

Changes

People are changing their attitudes. Have you noticed lately that more and more people with visible disabilities seem to be around? You see them on buses, at school, in restaurants, walking down the street, taking airplane flights, etc. *Is this because more people have disabilities now?* Possibly. But mainly it's because many people with visible disabilities are leaving their homes and hospitals and coming out into the world. They realize that they have as much right as anybody else to go places and do things. Laws have been passed that ensure there are:
- Ramps alongside stairs in front of buildings for people in wheelchairs.
- Parking spaces marked "Handicapped Only" close to doors at places like colleges, stores, and banks.
- Toilet stalls in public restrooms wide enough for a wheelchair.
- Educational services for all students with special needs.

What About You?

Have you looked closely at yourself to see what you consider to be your own strong points and weak points? You have both.

Think about yourself carefully now. Try to complete as many of these items as you can:

1. My personal strengths (talents, accomplishments, favorite activities, etc.): _____

_____

_____

_____

2. My personal weaknesses (disabilities, difficulties, limitations, things I don't know how to do yet, etc.): _____

_____

_____

_____

3. A challenge or disability I have overcome or I'm dealing with now: _____

_____

4. A positive way I can interact with a person with a disability.

_____

_____

Try This!

Many famous and accomplished people have, or have had, disabilities. Choose someone form the list that follows. **Investigate the life of this person** Find out what the person accomplished and how he or she coped with the disability.

Franklin D. Roosevelt – Crippled by Polio
Cher – Dyslexia
Christopher Reeve – Crippled in a riding accident
Thomas Edison – Learning disability
Helen Keller – Blind and deaf
Beethoven – Deaf
Marlee Matlin – Deaf
Robin Williams – ADHD
Stephen Hawking – Lou Gehrig's disease
Tom Cruise – Dyslexia
Magic Johnson – HIV
Michael J. Fox – Parkinson's disease

Interview a person with a disability in your school or community. Find out how he or she manages, and ways in which others can help.

Share what you learn with a friend, teammate, or group.

Decisions, Decisions

Small

Already today, you've made lots of decisions. You probably chose what to wear to school, how to comb your hair, and what you wanted to eat. These may not seem like big, important decisions, but they are still decisions. **See if you can list five other small decisions you've made today:**

1. _____

2. _____

3. _____

4. _____

5. _____

Big

Think of a big decision that you were aware of a person making recently. Briefly describe the decision here:

_____

Do you think you would have made the same decision if you were that person? *Why?*

_____

Describe a big decision you once made that had a good outcome:

_____

Describe a big decision you once made that had a bad outcome:

_____

Risky

Decision-making usually involves risk. Sometimes people get frustrated or scared about making a decision because they don't know what will happen after they decide. **Describe a time when you faced making a risky decision:**

_____

How Do You Make Decisions?

Look back at the decisions that you described on the previous page that had "good" and "bad" outcomes. Then read the following statements and put a **1** on the line in front of each statement that describes what happened when you made the "good" decision. Put a **2** on the line in front of each one that describes what happened when you made the "bad" decision. (Some statements won't fit either case.)

What conclusions can you draw concerning good and bad decision making from this exercise?

___At first I didn't realize I needed to make a decision.

___I waited until I was forced to decide.

___I decided on something that was really someone else's decision.

___I let someone else make my decision for me.

___I didn't try to please myself, but I did please other people.

___I didn't try to please anyone except myself.

___I didn't care who got hurt (including me).

___I thought over what would happen if I did several different things, and I chose the alternative that seemed best at the time.

___I flipped a coin (or something else of that nature).

___I didn't bother to get any information about possible choices.

___It seemed easier to jump in right away and make the decision than to think about it.

___I "just knew" what the best thing to do was, so I followed my intuition (hunch).

___I obtained as much information as I could get.

___I had a hunch what the best thing to do was. Nevertheless, I gathered the facts and thought it over before deciding.

___I talked over the situation with someone I trusted before deciding.

___I measured each alternative against my goals and chose the one that would get me closest to my goals.

___The decision I made was inconsistent with my personal values.

___My choices were limited by my skills (what I was capable of doing).

___My choices were limited by things outside myself (the environment).

___There were not many things I was willing to do, so my choices were limited.

___I was willing to do almost anything.

Decision Making

Getting What You Want

Decision-making is the process of selecting from two or more possible choices. A decision is not required unless there is more than one course of action to consider.

It is the individual who makes each decision unique. You and a friend may face similar decisions, but because you are different you may each want a different outcome. Learning decision-making skills increases the possibility that you can achieve what you want.

Each decision is limited by what you are *capable* of doing. If you cannot drive a car you can't choose between walking and driving. Your capability includes your knowledge of alternatives. If you are choosing a movie to see, but you don't know about certain movies that are playing, you cannot choose one of them.

Each decision is limited by the *environment*. If you are capable of driving a car, but don't have one available, you cannot choose to drive. If only one movie is playing where you are, you do not have a choice of movies.

Each decision is also limited by what you are *willing* to do. If you are willing to borrow or rent a car, you may increase your alternatives. If you are not willing to see a comedy or a foreign film, you restrict your movie choices. What you are willing to do is usually determined by what you **value** most.

So, to be a good decision-maker, you need to know:
1. Something about **yourself**—your values, and your capabilities.
2. Something about your **environment**—its opportunities, and its limitations.
3. How to **change** yourself and your environment—if they *can* be changed and if you *want* them changed.
4. The **skills** involved in the decision-making process. Learning these skills can help you become a skillful decision-maker.

The Process

Decision making is using what you know, or can learn, to get what you want. These are the steps involved:

1. Recognize and define the decision to be made.
2. Know what is important to you and what you want to achieve.
3. Examine the information you already have and seek and utilize new information.
4. Assess the risks and costs involved in choosing each alternative that is available.
5. Make the decision.
6. Develop a plan for putting the decision into action.

Decision or Outcome?

Have you ever made a poor decision? Try to think right now of one poor decision you have made. It could be the worst decision you ever made, or your most recent poor decision, or some "secret" poor decision. *Why do you consider it a poor decision?* _____
_____
_____

When most people say a decision is poor, they mean the result was not what they wanted. "It didn't turn out the way I thought it would." "Things didn't go right." Good decision-making *minimizes* the possibility of getting an unfavorable outcome, but it cannot *eliminate* the possibility. One of the first lessons in decision-making is to learn to make a distinction between a decision and its outcome.

A **decision** is the act of choosing from among several possibilities.

An **outcome** is the result or consequence of your decision.

You have direct control only over the decision, not the outcome. If you make a good decision, it will not guarantee a good outcome, because you cannot completely control the outcome. However, learning how to make good decisions will increase your chances of getting good outcomes.

Remember that the "goodness" of a decision is based on how it is made, not on how it turns out. For example, imagine that a coin is to be tossed, and you are to call heads or tails. If you call the toss correctly, you win $50; if you don't, you win nothing. You decide to call heads. The toss is tails. *Did you make a good or poor decision? Why?*

_____
_____
_____

The Decision Agent

When it's especially important to make a good decision, people often ask someone to help them. They might use a stockbroker, a lawyer, a doctor, or an architect for certain difficult decisions. **Imagine a new kind of expert.** Instead of a stockbroker who is an expert on investments, or an architect who is an expert on designing, assume that there is a **"decision agent"**—an expert on decision making. You can employ a decision agent to make your decisions for you.

To learn something about yourself and about the decisions that are important to you, answer the questions to the right. Then, get together with a classmate and discuss your answers—and the reasoning behind them.

Assume your city has a limited number of decision agents. You can assign only three decisions in your life to the agent. *Which three would you assign?*

1. _____
2. _____
3. _____

Assume that your city requires you to assign *all* of the decisions in your life *except* three to a decision agent. *Which three would you not assign?*

1. _____
2. _____
3. _____

For each decision in the first question, what instruction would you give your decision agent? Why?

Know Where You're Going

I'D LIKE TO STUDY MEDICINE... BE A GREAT SURGEON... ...OR AN ATTORNEY DEFENDING THE UNDERDOG AGAINST THE ESTABLISHMENT...

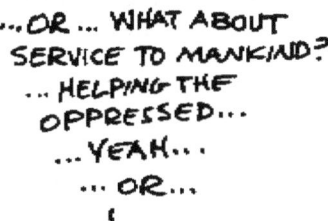

...OR... WHAT ABOUT SERVICE TO MANKIND?... HELPING THE OPPRESSED... ...YEAH... ...OR...

...OR... MAYBE I CAN GET A JOB AS A BOX-BOY DOWN AT THE MARKET ON THE CORNER.

When Alice in Wonderland was trying to decide which way to go in the wood, she asked the Cheshire Cat:

"Would you tell me, please, which way I ought to go from here?"
"That depends a good deal on where you want to get to," said the Cat.
"I don't much care where—" said Alice.
"Then it doesn't matter which way you go," said the Cat.

If you don't know where you're going, then it really doesn't matter which choice you make. However, if you *do* know where you're going, then what you decide matters very much.

Decision-making has been described as using what you know to get what you want. This means you must know what you want. Strangely enough, many people are not sure what they want. It is not always easy to say what you value. Values change, and sometimes they conflict.

Do you know what you want?

What Would You Do If...

- You were the President of the United States.

- You were given $1,000,000.

- You could do anything you wanted for one year.

How Values Affect Decisions

CATHY'S CHOICE—Cathy has been offered two promising jobs. Being a skilled decision-maker, she knows the following:

A. Alternatives
She has three choices:
1. Choose job A.
2. Choose job B.
3. Don't choose either job.

B. Values
Cathy values the following in a job, listed in order of importance:
1. Large income
2. Security
3. Advancement opportunities

C. Probabilities
Chances of achieving a job that satisfies these values are as follows:

1. Job A offers her a 25% chance of a very large income and advancement opportunities, however, the environment is very competitive and there is a 75% chance that she will not be able to stay in the job.

2. Job B offers her a 50% chance of a fairly large income with few advancement opportunities and a 50% chance of not performing well enough to stay in the job.

3. Choosing neither job offers an unknown chance of finding a better job.

What would Cathy decide? _____

Why? _____

What would you decide and why? _____

What other information would help Cathy? _____

Would it help for her to list more specific objectives? _____

Would it help to know how much more important a large income is than security? _____

How should Cathy decide how much risk to take? _____

What difference would it make if Cathy were:
1. rich? _____
2. poor? _____
3. married? _____
4. experienced? _____
5. talented? _____
6. happy? _____
7. older? _____

The Informed Decision

Knowing What to Know

Decisions are based on what you know *and* what you want. People make different decisions because they have different values (wants) and because they possess different information.

What you *know* is determined by the information you *have* and the information you *collect*. After you have collected information and evaluated it, you can better judge the degree of risk involved in various decisions you might make. And you can predict more accurately your chances of achieving the outcome you desire.

Here are four kinds of mistakes commonly made by people when they gather information before making a decision. *Have you made some of these mistakes? Have your friends? Can you think of other examples?*

A. **Not knowing alternatives.**
1. Susan does not apply for a scholarship because she doesn't know it exists.
2. Eric's dad pays $620 for a T.V. because he doesn't know that the same set sells for $549 at another store.

B. **Not knowing possible outcomes.**
1. Lee decides to take a cold medicine without knowing its side effects, gets drowsy, and falls asleep in class.
2. Sandra goes to college in another state without considering how much she will miss her family and friends.

C. **Misinterpreting the importance of information.**
1. Celia misses the student council meeting because she hears a rumor that it has been canceled.
2. Ross decides to buy an old car because the owner, who is a stranger to him, says it is in good condition.

D. **Collecting useless, irrelevant information.**
1. Alex collects information about software programs that are not compatible with his computer.
2. Jose decides to become a real estate agent based on career information that is obsolete.
3. Marla spends several hours talking to salespeople about cars that are out of her price range.

Building Information Power

Lauren is currently employed in a sales job that she took immediately after completing high school. The job pays well and Lauren enjoys her work, but wants to be eligible to advance to the position of sales trainer. Her coworkers have told her that to do so she must have a degree from a two-year college. Lauren is engaged to be married and her fiancée wants her to continue her education, preferably at a four-year college. However, her boss has confirmed that she needs only two years of college. Lauren's friends think that she must decide for herself—and that she should consider the uncertainty of giving up a well-paying job for only the promise of advancement opportunities. In giving a great deal of thought to the decision, Lauren identifies the following sources of information that can help her decide whether to continue her education by going to a two- or four-year college.

Things to think about:
1. Her talents, skills, and abilities
2. What work-related things are most important to her
3. What life style she wants in the future
4. What her short-term and long-range goals are
5. What outcome she can expect if she gets more education
6. What other people she cares for want her to do
7. How well her existing job matches her values and goals

People to talk to:
8. Fiancée   9. Friends   10. Parents   11. Boss
12. College counselor   13. Sales trainers at her company

Things to read:
14. College catalogs   15. Occupational information
16. Job market data (present and future) for her present job
17. Reports on jobs available to college graduates

Things to do:
18. Send for and complete college application forms
19. Visit two- and four-year colleges she might attend
20. Assess financial needs
21. Take any college entrance and placement tests that are required

If you were to help Lauren choose three of the best sources of information, which three would you choose?

Number____ Why?_____

Number____ Why?_____

Number____ Why?_____

Now, think of an issue that YOU need to decide in the next few weeks or months. Choose a fairly important one. Describe it here:

_____
_____
_____
_____

What sources of information can YOU consult in order to decide what to do?

Things to think about:

1._____

2._____

3._____

People to talk to:

1._____

2._____

3._____

Things to read:

1._____

2._____

3._____

Things to do:

1._____

2._____

3._____

Decisions & Consequences

Risk-Taking

One of the most difficult things about making decisions is that you can never be certain how things will turn out. If you could predict the outcome of every choice you made before you acted, deciding would be easier. You would still need to decide which outcome you preferred, but you would not have to worry about risks.

Unfortunately, your environment is uncertain. It is also complex, dynamic, and sometimes competitive. Some people deal with uncertainties and risks by ignoring them. You will be doing yourself a big favor if, instead, you develop skills for making the best decisions possible. As a skilled decision-maker, you can at least increase the *probability* of getting favorable outcomes.

Assess Yourself!

Do you usually: ____ *Take risks?* ____ *Play it safe?*

Suppose you are given the following choice of risk:
A_1. A 100% chance of winning $5 thousand.
A_2. A 10% chance of winning $5 million.

Which would you choose? ____A_1 ____A_2 *Why?* _____

_____

Suppose you are given the following choice of risk:
B_1. A 10% chance of winning $5 million.
     A 90% chance of winning nothing.
B_2. An 11% chance of winning $1 million.
     An 89% chance of winning nothing.

Which would you choose? ____B_1 ____B_2 *Why?* _____

_____

3. *Which choices would most people make?*

_____

5. *What factors determine your willingness to take risks?*

_____

_____

Predicting Outcomes

One of the steps in the decision-making process is looking ahead to see what could happen as a result of each choice you might make. It is important to think about the possible consequences of each alternative action. This is called "predicting."

Sometimes it is possible to gather information to help you predict. Sometimes you must predict based only on what you already know. Making accurate predictions takes practice. The better you are at predicting possible outcomes, the more likely you are to make decisions whose outcomes please you.

What's Your Prediction?

What Would Happen If...

1. You did not go to college? _____

2. You never got married? _____

3. You joined the military? _____

4. You studied at least 3 hours every day? _____

5. You became a teenage parent? _____

6. You became a lawyer? _____

7. You lived on welfare? _____

8. You got married tomorrow? _____

9. You dropped out of high school? _____

10. You became a professional entertainer? _____

Discuss your predictions with a classmate. Answer these questions: *How did you make your predictions? What information did you use?*

Now Try This

List five possible actions that you might take and predict an outcome for each. List actions you've considered and some your parents or friends have suggested.

What Would Happen If...

1. Action: _____

Outcome: _____

2. Action: _____

Outcome: _____

3. Action: _____

Outcome: _____

4. Action: _____

Outcome: _____

5. Action: _____

Outcome: _____

Discuss your predictions with a classmate. Answer these questions:
- *What did you learn about yourself?*
- *Do you think your answers will be different in 5 years? Why?*

Critical Decisions

Larry has been a fairly good student throughout high school. He has talked increasingly about going to a local university and majoring in political science and international relations.

Larry's father left the family several years ago and has never provided financial support. He now lives in Europe. Larry's mother is the sole support of his younger brother and sister. Four years ago, Larry moved in with his aunt and younger cousin. His aunt works as a customer service representative for a small mail-order company. The aunt has had a series of medical problems over the past year including a major operation. She was released from her job for several months because of her illness, but can go back whenever she is well enough, probably in about a month.

Now, in his senior year of high school, Larry has decided to attend a junior college and study restaurant management. He plans to go to work as a waiter as soon as he can get a job in a local restaurant. Larry has discussed this decision at length with his counselor. He feels that, since his aunt has devoted several years to him and now is ill, he should be prepared to take over the support of the family at any time. He is desperately afraid that if he goes to the university as planned, his aunt will end up on welfare. This is very unlikely, since the aunt will soon be able to return to work; however, right after his father left, Larry's family experienced a year on welfare and Larry has never forgotten it.

Larry's counselor has suggested that Larry apply to the university anyway, since his chances of gaining admission and financial aid seem quite good. Larry refuses to fill out applications for four-year colleges or to discuss the situation any further. He says he can always go to college later. His aunt's response to Larry's decision is, "Well, whatever he wants to do..."

Questions

1. *Why has Larry decided as he has?* _____

2. *What effect might his decision have on his long-range goals?* _____

3. *Has he made a good decision? Why?* _____

4. *Has he considered all the alternatives? What others would you suggest to him?* _____

Imagine That...

You have one year left in high school. You are exactly who you are in real life, with your present grades, abilities, habits, activities, and home life. Suddenly, you are forced to leave school and be entirely on your own. You must support yourself in any way you can, with no help from your parents. *What could you do to support yourself?* **Describe three possibilities:**

1. _____
_____

2. _____
_____

3. _____
_____

Circle any possibilities on your list that would satisfy you for 10 years.

Now imagine that, instead of being on your own immediately, you learn that you will be completely on your own a year from now. *Knowing that you have one year in which to prepare before you are on your own, what plans can you make? What actions can you take to get ready for next year? What information can you get that you do not have now?* **Write your answers below.**

PLANS: _____
_____
_____

ACTIONS: _____
_____
_____

INFORMATION: _____
_____
_____

Evaluate

If you do all these things, what opportunities will you gain during the year that you have to prepare?

1. _____
_____
_____

2. _____
_____
_____

3. _____
_____
_____

How much will your future be changed if you don't do anything different from what you are doing now?

_____
_____
_____
_____
_____
_____
_____

Solving Problems

Mazes...

How do you react when you're upset about a problem? Do you:
___ stop and think, then act?
___ blame others?
___ blame yourself?
___ strike back?
___ run away?
___ bottle up your feelings?
___ do the same thing over and over again?
___ talk it over with another person?

Why do some people really suffer when they have problems, while others seem to be able to tackle and solve them easily?

Some people see their problems as traps, with no way out. Others see their problems as mazes—tough maybe, but not impossible. **The truth is: there are a lot of mazes in life, but very few traps.**

...Not Traps!

Take a look at this list of problem areas. Circle all items that remind you of *your* problems:

- Being accepted by friends
- Becoming independent
- Being an individual
- Living with controls and restrictions
- Being understood by your parents and/or other adults
- Getting along with authority figures
- Making decisions
- Clothes
- Alcohol and/or other drugs
- Your identity
- Accepting responsibility
- Being alone
- Temptations
- Lack of privileges
- Grades
- Your appearance
- A school subject or class
- Events/conditions in the U.S.
- World events/conditions
- Sex
- Money
- Your body
- Other _____

Choose one of the items you circled and describe the problem here: _____

_____

_____

_____

_____

Steps for Solving a Problem Responsibly

Following these steps will see you through the maze of almost any problem. Practice them now by working out a solution to the problem you described on the previous page.

1. Stop all blaming. Blaming someone (including yourself) for the problem will not solve it. If you really want to solve the problem, put your energy into working out a solution. Blaming yourself and others is a waste of time.

2. Define the problem. Start by asking yourself two questions: "What exactly is the problem?" and "Whose problem is it?" If you find that it's not your problem, let the people who "own" the problem solve it themselves. Or ask them "How can I help?"

3. Consider asking for help. Once you are sure that *you* own the problem, decide whether or not to discuss it with someone else. Choose a person who will *really listen*, not just give advice.

4. Think of alternative solutions. Ask yourself: "What are some things I could do about this?" Think of as many reasonable ideas for solving the problem as possible. *To do this, you will probably need to collect some information.*

5. Evaluate the alternatives. For each idea you come up with, ask yourself: "What will happen to me and the other people involved if I try this one?" Be very honest with yourself. If you don't know how someone will be affected, ask that person, "How would you feel if I... ."

6. Make a decision. Choose the alternative that appears to have the best chance of succeeding. If your solution is a responsible one, it won't hurt anyone unnecessarily—and will probably work.

7. Follow through. After you've made the decision, stick to it for a reasonable length of time. If the decision doesn't work, try another alternative. If the decision *does* work, but causes additional problems in the process, start all over again to solve them.

The problem is: _____
_____
_____

Alternatives: _____
_____
_____
_____
_____
_____
_____

Decision: _____
_____

Follow-through steps:

1. _____
2. _____
3. _____
4. _____

Things to Try:

Watch a T.V. show and notice what problem the main actor or actress is trying to solve. Watch how the problem is handled. Then decide in your own mind if it was handled in a responsible way. (Or do this with a story.) Discuss it with a friend.

Listen to a friend. Next time a friend of yours has a problem, ask him or her: "Would you like to talk about it?" Then spend most of your time listening. See what happens if you give very little or no advice at all.

Follow the steps. Next time you have a problem, ask a friend to help you use these "Steps for Solving a Problem Responsibly." Keep notes and take as much time as you need to gather information. Offer to help your friend with a problem, too.

Know Your Goals!

Accomplishments...

Some people look at life as a game—one big game made up of many little games. The object of all the little games, and the big one too, is to win. And just as in a baseball or soccer game, you win when you **know your goals**. You also win when you recognize your accomplishments and feel good about them. Knowing you can succeed makes it easier to take advantage of opportunities and to find ways around and over the roadblocks in your life. You come out a winner! Unlike baseball and soccer, when it comes to the game of life, nobody has to be a loser!

You accomplish a great deal every day. You think, make decisions, go places, and do things—and much of the time you interact with other people in the process. Many of your accomplishments are small, but they are *still* accomplishments.

You can also take credit for some very big important accomplishments. Think of the years of school you've completed. You've learned to read and write, and to solve many kinds of problems. *You have a right to be proud of yourself!*

Think of something small you've accomplished today. What was it? _____

_____

_____

Now think of a bigger accomplishment—something you've done within the past three years What was it?

_____

_____

Accomplishments are goals you've already met!

...and Goals

Goals—what are they anyway?

Usually a goal is an **outcome**—an end result. A goal is something to shoot for.

A goal might be to *have* something, like a new outfit, a car, or money. A goal might be to *achieve* something, such as high school graduation, a job as an astronaut, financial security, or a thorough understanding of computer technology. To be a better friend, a better learner, or a better cook are also examples of goals.

Some goals are short term, and others are long range. Short-term goals are outcomes that you can achieve fairly quickly. For example, deciding to make an important phone call this afternoon, complete your homework before tomorrow, clean your room on Saturday, finish your

Goals, cont.

chores by noon, and repair your bike by next Thursday are all short-term goals.

Long-range goals are formulated with the understanding that they will not be achieved until several months or years from now. When you decide to travel to Europe after you graduate, attend a particular college or technical school, save money toward the purchase of a car, or become a television director, you have established a long-range goal. **In the spaces below, take a minute to write down some of your current goals:**

Put to the Test

Choose one short-term or long-range goal from the chart below and answer these questions as honestly as you can:

Goal: _____

_____

1. Did *you* decide to set this goal, or did someone else talk you into it? _____

2. How do you feel about having this goal? _____

_____

3. Is your goal realistic (one you can attain)? _____

_____

4. Did setting this goal cause you any frustration or conflict?

_____

5. How much risk-taking is involved in reaching this goal?

_____

6. Did you get advice from anyone else before you decided on this goal? From whom?

_____

My Goals

SHORT-TERM	TARGET DATE/PLAN
School: _____	_____
_____	_____
Family: _____	_____
_____	_____
Personal: _____	_____
_____	_____
LONG-RANGE	
Educational: _____	_____
_____	_____
Job/Career: _____	_____
_____	_____
Financial: _____	_____
_____	_____
Personal: _____	_____
_____	_____

Control Your Time

One of the hardest things about attaining goals—particularly long-range goals—is making time to do what's needed to reach them.

You're probably pretty good at reaching short-term goals. You do it every day. One reason is that short-term goals usually have short-term deadlines. If you don't make that phone call this afternoon, you won't know if your plans for tomorrow are on or off. If you don't finish your homework early, you won't be able to watch T.V. If you don't repair your bike before the weekend, the Saturday morning ride is off.

Long-range goals often don't have deadlines at all. At least not at first. Instead, they require careful planning and the completion of lots of small tasks. Going to Europe after graduation, for example, involves earning and saving money, making travel arrangements, getting a passport, deciding where to go, what to see, how to travel, where to stay, and whom to go with, just for starters.

A long-range goal without a plan is just a dream. Try to get in the habit of writing down all the steps required to reach a goal. Then start taking those steps right away. Even if your goal is five years down the road, there are things that you can do about it now!

Getting control of your time will allow you to take daily, weekly, or monthly steps toward your long-range goals.

Imagine that the circle below represents a typical day in your life. It is already divided into four parts, so each quarter represents 6 hours in your day. **Using dotted lines, further subdivide the quarters of the circle to represent parts of your day.**

Make a "Day Pie"

Estimate how many hours or parts of hours you spend in school, sleeping, doing homework, earning money, eating, watching T.V., playing, reading, working, and other things. Label each piece of your "day pie" to show the major activity it represents. Once you've completed the pie, take a good look at it.

Are you satisfied with how you spend your time?

Where can you fit in the steps you must take to reach your long-range goals?

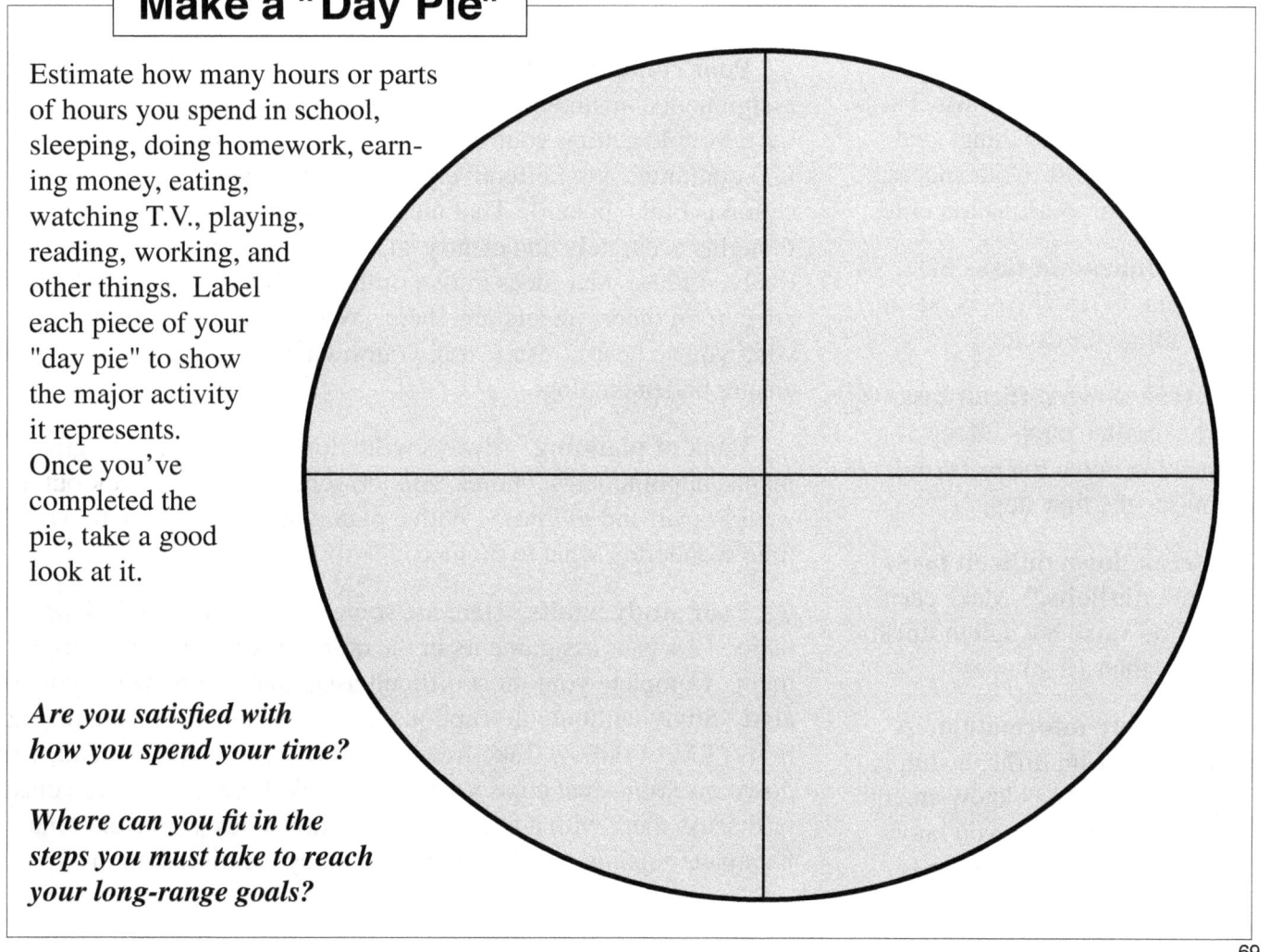

Time-wasters

Consider this:

*You waste your time whenever you spend it doing something **less** important when you could be doing something **more** important.*

To determine whether or not an activity is a time-waster *for you*, measure it against your goals. Is the activity helping you reach your goals? If not, how can you reduce or eliminate the time you devote to it?

Procrastination

Most of us tend to put off things that are **unpleasant**, things that are **difficult**, and things that involve **tough decisions**. These are often the very things that contribute most to our success! Try these procrastination cures:

- **Do unpleasant tasks first.** Or do them in small pieces, setting a deadline for each.

- **Break down difficult tasks into smaller parts.** Keep breaking down the parts until you see the first step.

- **Break down difficult tasks into "minijobs."** Make each minijob small enough to finish in less than 10 minutes.

- **Get more information.** A task may seem difficult simply because you don't know enough about it. The more you know, the more likely you are to become interested and involved.

Check Yours!

___**Telephone/Texting.** If you are frequently interrupted by phone calls or text messages while studying or working on an important project, try asking your friends to contact you at an agreed-upon hour. Set aside a special time each day to call or text, too. Limit each call to a few minutes.

___**Television.** It's okay to watch your favorite shows, but don't watch T.V. just to fill (or kill) time. Instead, use that time to do something that will move you in the direction of a goal!

___**Cluttered room, work area, or desk.** How much time do you waste looking for misplaced items? Not very many people can do their best work amid disorganization. Take some time to "shape up" your space. Have at hand all necessary tools and materials. For studying, you'll need such things as books, paper, pens, pencils, calculator, notebooks, notes, erasers, dictionary, and software.

___**Socializing.** Being with friends is important, but try not to let socializing distract you from other things that you've decided to do. When you plan your day, allow ample time for enjoyable interaction with friends and family. Then, when it's time to work on other goals, don't socialize.

___**Poor communication.** If you frequently fail to understand your assignments, misinterpret statements made by friends or family, or have trouble getting your own ideas across, put some extra effort into communicating effectively. Over 90 percent of all communication is oral (spoken). That means you need to 1) state your own thoughts accurately and clearly, and 2) listen actively and attentively. Phrase your ideas in two or three different ways until you are certain others understand them. When listening, paraphrase what you've heard (restate it in your own words) or ask questions to ensure understanding.

___**Lack of planning.** Always write down your goals, assignments, appointments, chores, and job schedule. Then work out a weekly plan and *follow it*. With a plan, you'll never have to waste time wondering what to do next.

___**Poor study habits.** Here are some tips: Study at a desk or table. List your assignments in the order in which you plan to do them. Complete your most difficult assignments first while you are alert. Study without interruptions (phone calls/texting) and distractions (T.V. or radio). Take frequent short breaks. As you read, write down questions that cross your mind. Ask those questions in class or discuss them with a friend. Periodically study with a classmate. Complete reading assignments before they are discussed in class.

Take Charge!

Out of Control?

Have you ever lost control? Have you ever deliberately broken something or yelled at someone and then asked yourself, "Why did I do that?"

Think of a time when you lost control and describe it here: ___

___

___

___

It's bad enough that you can't control everything that happens to you. It's even worse when you can't control *you*. You aren't alone. Most people have trouble controlling themselves at times.

Sometimes we lose control when we don't really understand what we are feeling. When you are aware of your emotions, you are better able to take charge of yourself and what is happening. When you accept your feelings, you realize that they are neither right nor wrong. Feelings just are. They are part of being human.

What feelings led up to the situation you described above? ___

___

___

___

Try This:

Practice being assertive. Don't let negative feelings build up inside you. If you don't like something, say so. When you disagree with someone, state your own opinion. It's not necessary to put others down. Just say, "I feel..." or "This is what I believe... ."

Keep a journal. At the end of each day, list some of the ways you controlled yourself. Discover your ability to handle situations. Write down any strong feelings you had that day, too, and how you expressed them.

Talk to someone about your feelings. When you feel angry, resentful, jealous, or cheated, share your emotions (and what caused them) with someone who will *really listen* to you.

Imaginary Barriers

Sometimes people *stop* themselves from doing things. Later, they ask themselves, "Why *didn't* I do that?"

Describe a time when you stopped yourself from doing something that you really wanted to do.

_____
_____
_____

What stopped you? _____
_____
_____
_____

What Holds You Back?

Make a list of the things you want to do (or stop doing). Then, describe any worries, fears, or habits that are getting in your way.

What I want to try:	Ways I block myself:
1. _____	_____
_____	_____
_____	_____
2. _____	_____
_____	_____
_____	_____
3. _____	_____
_____	_____
_____	_____

Do It Anyway

If you speak up in front of everyone,
You may feel embarrassed.
Speak up anyway!

Success may cause
People to be jealous of you.
Succeed anyway!

Being a leader may cause
People to resist you.
Be a leader anyway!

It's scary if you try something new.
You may make a mistake or feel awkward.
Try new things anyway!

If you make yourself look good,
People might stare at you.
Take good care of yourself anyway!

If you do what you want to do
Instead of what your friends want you to do,
They may get mad at you.
Do what you decide to do anyway!

If you disagree with others,
They may not like you anymore.
Say what you think anyway!

If you take a rest
In the middle of an active day,
You may feel guilty.
Relax anyway!

You might feel silly
If you start to cry.
Let out hurt feelings and
Get rid of them anyway!

Assertiveness

"AGGRESSIVE"   "PASSIVE"   "ASSERTIVE"

Aggressive

Aggressive people:
• intentionally attack, take advantage of, humiliate, hurt, put down, or depreciate other people.
• act on the belief that others are not as important as they are.

The aggressive person's mottos are:
  "Get them before they get me."
  "How you play doesn't count, only that you win."
  "Never give a sucker an even break."

Example:
As you leave a store after purchasing something, you realize that you have been shortchanged 95 cents. **You hurry back into the store and loudly demand 95 cents, adding a derogatory comment about cashiers who can't add.**

Passive

Passive people:
• permit others to take advantage of them.
• discount themselves and act as if others are more important than they are.

The passive person's mottos are:
  "I should never make anyone feel uncomfortable, resentful, or displeased, except myself."
  "I should never disappoint anyone or cause anyone to disapprove of me."

Example:
As you leave a store after purchasing something, you realize that you have been shortchanged 95 cents. **You pause to decide if 95 cents is worth the effort. After a few moments of indecision, you decide not to cause a hassle, and leave.**

Assertive

Assertive people:
• express themselves openly and honestly to communicate their needs, wants, or feelings, without discounting the wants, needs or feelings of others.
• act according to the belief that all people including themselves, are important.

The assertive person's mottos are:
  "I have the right to ask for what I want."
  "Others have an equal right to ask for what they want."

Example:
As you leave a store, you realize that you have been shortchanged 95 cents. **You go back, get the attention of the clerk, display the change you received, and state that you were shortchanged 95 cents.**

More Examples

Circle the label that fits.

1. You are at a concert. A man sits down next to you and begins to smoke. The smoke really bothers you.

a. You suffer in silence, figuring that if he wants to smoke, that's his right.
Aggressive Passive Assertive

b. You become very hostile, and demand that he move or stop smoking—or else.
Aggressive Passive Assertive

c. You firmly but politely tell him the effect the smoke is having on you. You ask him to refrain from smoking or to sit in another seat.
Aggressive Passive Assertive

2. A person you dated once calls and asks you out. Your first date wasn't much fun, and you don't want to go out with him/her again.

a. You accept, do not enjoy yourself and, still unwilling to be honest, leave yourself open to being asked out again.
Aggressive Passive Assertive

b. You tell him/her that you felt uncomfortable on the last date and would prefer not to go out again, and you thank him/her for asking.
Aggressive Passive Assertive

c. You say, "You've got to be kidding! I couldn't stand another date with you."
Aggressive Passive Assertive

How Do You Respond?

As you've been reading and writing, you've probably thought of situations in which *you* reacted aggressively, passively, or assertively. Perhaps you:
— wanted someone to leave you alone.
— were trying to resist a salesperson.
— wanted to deny someone's request to borrow an item from you.
— disagreed with someone.
— wanted to tell someone you were being treated unfairly.

On the chart, briefly describe situations you've experienced, how you felt at the time each situation occurred, whether your behavior was aggressive, passive, or assertive, and how things turned out. Ask yourself: *Could I have been more assertive?* **Discuss your answers with a classmate.**

The Situation	Your Behavior: Aggressive, Passive, or Assertive	The Outcome

Influence

Who Influences You?

Has anybody ever caused you to do something without ordering or forcing you to do it? Answer carefully.

You may think that the answer to that question is no, but if you do, you are almost certainly wrong!

People *do* cause others to do things without force. It happens every day. And it even happens to you. The way it happens is called *influence*.

No matter how independent you are or how able you are to make your own decisions, you are still influenced in some ways by other people.

For example:
- The good looking guy in the T.V. commercial says your hair will look great if you use Peach Cloud shampoo. Next time you need some shampoo, you buy Peach Cloud.
- All of your friends are wearing a certain kind of shoe. The next time you are in a store that sells shoes, you buy a pair.
- A particular candidate for class president says more things that you like than any of the other candidates. On election day, you vote for her.
- You do something that your friends urge you to do, even though you think it is wrong.

Influences can cause you to:
—imitate someone.
—buy a product.
—think a certain way.
—behave a certain way.
—look a certain way.

To what extent do certain people influence you? On the scales at the right, rate the people named according to how much they influence you—**1** is low influence, **5** is high influence. Before you decide, look again at the definition of influence.

Rating Scales

- a special friend your age

  1 |—|—|—|—| 5

- a favorite singer/musician

  1 |—|—|—|—| 5

- a famous athlete

  1 |—|—|—|—| 5

- a favorite teacher

  1 |—|—|—|—| 5

- an older friend

  1 |—|—|—|—| 5

- a movie or T.V. actor or actress

  1 |—|—|—|—| 5

- a political leader

  1 |—|—|—|—| 5

- a minister, priest, or rabbi

  1 |—|—|—|—| 5

- a special adult friend

  1 |—|—|—|—| 5

- your parent(s)

  1 |—|—|—|—| 5

Ratings, cont.

Look back at the rating scales. *Which people on the list have a positive influence on you most of the time?*

_____

_____

Which people have a negative influence on you most of the time?

_____

_____

Describe a time when you decided not to let someone influence you.

_____

_____

_____

_____

_____

Think of someone who has the kind of influence on you that you want. *Who is it?*

_____

How is this person a good influence?

_____

_____

_____

How Ads Influence

Watch T.V. and internet commercials with a different eye. Remember, these people are trying to influence your behavior. They will go to great lengths to get you to buy their products. Here are some techniques commonly used in advertising:

1. Testimonial: Someone famous testifies that he or she uses the product; you conclude that the product must be good if this person likes it.

2. Bandwagon: The ad suggests that "everyone" is using the product; therefore, if you don't want to be left out, you must purchase it, too.

3. Sense Appeal: The ad works by stimulating one or more of the five senses, like vision, hearing, or taste.

4. Transfer: The person selling the product is good-looking, sexy, a great dresser, famous, etc. You imagine (often without realizing it) that you will acquire the same qualities if you use the product.

5. Generalities: The ad uses words like the "greatest," the "best," the "only," but doesn't back up those words with facts.

6. Weasel Words: The advertiser says things like, "brighter teeth," "less filling," "more pain relief," or "will help reduce tension." These little words suggest a lot, but mean little. They don't tell you, for example, "brighter than what?" or "more pain relief than what?" The words allow advertisers to "weasel out" of their responsibility to give facts.

7. Plain Folks: These ads use average looking people to appeal to the average buyer. You feel as though you can trust these people.

8. Humor: People often remember an ad that is funny and makes them laugh. The laughter creates good feelings that pay off later, when you choose what to buy.

9. Stacking the Deck: Only the good things about a product are described, while the less attractive or bad features are ignored.

10. Opinions Stated as Facts: This type of ad often uses a well known and respected person or a powerful voice to sell the product. Because of the person's image, the opinions she or he states come across as facts.

Pressure!

Positive and Negative

One of the strongest influences on people is pressure. Pressure can take many forms. Sometimes pressure is positive. For example, a teacher pressures students to study, learn, and get good grades. A supervisor pressures employees to conform to high performance standards. Sometimes we put this kind of pressure on ourselves.

Other times pressure is negative. For example, an individual pressures a friend to use alcohol or other drugs. One teenager pressures another to go somewhere "off limits." A group pressures its members to participate in an illegal demonstration.

Negative pressure can put you in a "no-win" situation. You don't know whether to do what the person wants or not. If you *don't* do it, you risk losing a friendship. If you *do*, you hurt yourself. Either way you lose—or so it seems.

In situations like these, try to decide what's most important to you. Does a real friend constantly pressure you to be somebody you aren't or to do things you don't want to do? Should you give in to people who put you in that kind of position?

You must choose when to stand your ground. Ask yourself these questions:
1. What am I being asked to do?
2. Do I really want to do it?
3. What are the consequences of doing it?
4. What other choices do I have?

Remember a time someone pressured you to *be somebody* other than yourself. *How did you feel?* _____
_____
_____

What did you do? _____
_____

Recall a time when someone pressured you to *do something* you knew was wrong or dangerous. *How did you feel?*
_____
_____
_____

What did you do? _____
_____

All Dressed Up

Peer pressure comes in many styles and disguises. It can be:
- friendly
- teasing
- intimidating
- guilt-producing
- humiliating
- verbally abusive
- demanding
- bribing
- threatening
- physically menacing

What style of peer pressure do you recognize in each of these statements?

"I'll take out the trash for a week if you'll..."
Style: _____

"If you know what's good for you, you'll..."
Style: _____

"If you were really my friend, you'd..."
Style: _____

"Come on, be a pal and ..."
Style: _____

"If you don't do it, I'll tell Mom."
Style: _____

"It's okay, we all know you can't handle your liquor."
Style: _____

"Only a wimpy, blubber-faced loser like you would refuse this stuff."
Style: _____

Ways to Say No

1. **Say no.** Clearly, flatly, confidently.
2. **Say no and give a reason.** "No thanks. Smoking is bad for me and makes me look stupid."
3. **Say no and suggest something else to do.** "No thanks. I'm hungry. Want to go for a pizza?"
4. **Say no and leave.** "No thanks. See you around."

Ways To Be Convincing

- **Always respond to peer pressure assertively.** When pressured in a friendly way, remember that you too can be friendly—even humorous—yet assertive at the same time.
- **Use appropriate voice and body language.**
    1. Maintain good posture.
    2. Establish eye contact.
    3. Let your facial expression project calm confidence.
    4. Speak clearly, in a firm, steady voice.
    5. Be definite. Don't say, "I probably shouldn't" or "I don't think so."
    6. Avoid debate. If your first two or three refusals are ignored, get away. Don't put up with attempts to persuade.
- **When you say no and give a reason, use only a few words.** Don't spend a lot of time explaining yourself. Remember, you have a right to make your own decisions.
- **When pressure is intimidating or menacing, don't waste time arguing or talking.** Leave the scene as quickly as possible. If you think you are in danger, find someone who can help you.

Try It!

One of your best friends has gradually stopped calling and coming over. Lately, when you see this friend at school, he or she is with a group of kids you don't know. You decide to stop by your friend's house one afternoon to see what's up. Your friend seems happy to see you, and invites you upstairs to his or her room where you encounter several members of the new group sitting around smoking dope and drinking beer. Your friend teasingly invites you to "relax, for once" and join them.
What do you say?
_____
_____

What do you do?
_____

Responsibility

You Are Responsible

What does it mean to be responsible? A lot of people who think that they aren't very responsible—really are. By not focusing on how often they do responsible things, they sell themselves short. Maybe that's how it is with you.

We usually hear about it when we've done something *irresponsible*. But when we do *responsible* things, nobody says anything. We're *expected* to behave responsibly, right?

Let's try a little experiment. First, answer this question:

Are you a responsible person?
___Yes   ___No

Now, answer these questions:

Did you get yourself out of bed this morning?
___Yes   ___No

Did you fix all or part of your breakfast?
___Yes   ___No

Did you do what was necessary to get to school?
___Yes   ___No

Were you on time to class?
___Yes   ___No

Have you done something helpful or constructive lately?
___Yes   ___No

Have you kept your word during the past week—done the things you said you would do?
___Yes   ___No

Have you admitted you were wrong at least once during the past week?
___Yes   ___No

Count your "Yes" answers and your "No" answers, and then look at the first question again. *Are you a responsible person?*

What is responsibility? The word itself provides an important clue.
  response - ability

The ability to respond or get involved.

To Earth

You are responsible as a creature of planet Earth. All of the living things on our planet relate to and depend on each other. We live in *ecological* balance. Humans have a great responsibility to maintain that balance. Sadly, we have at times neglected that responsibility.

List three things about our planet that **concern you**.

1. _____

2. _____

3. _____

Now list your ideas for improving Earth's **natural environment.** They can be big things, like developing a non-fossil fuel, or little things, like conserving water.

1. _____

2. _____

3. _____

To Others

You can be a responsible member of a group.

You can use your power to affect other people in groups to which you belong. Whether the group is your family, some friends, a class, or a church group, you can treat people the way you like to be treated.

Describe a time recently when you did something on your own that **benefited a group**.

_____

_____

Describe a time when you **kept your promise** to someone, even though it was hard.

_____

_____

Describe a time recently when you **admitted that you made a mistake** or forgot something.

_____

_____

Describe a time when you **stopped doing something** so that someone wouldn't get hurt.

_____

_____

Describe a time when you **included someone** in an activity who would otherwise have been left out.

_____

_____

To Yourself

You can be responsible to yourself.

You have a right to be the most important person in your own world. Not only is it your right to like and take care of yourself, it's your most important job in life. Being responsible begins with being in charge of yourself. What good does it do to be able to respond to ecological situations or to others when you aren't able to respond to yourself?

Here are two stories about responsiblity.

I'LL DECIDE!

Sydney Harris, a newspaper columnist, walked with a friend to a newsstand near the friend's office. His companion greeted the newsstand attendant in a very friendly way, but in return received gruff and discourteous service.

Accepting the newspaper that was shoved rudely in his direction, the friend politely smiled and wished the attendant a nice weekend. As the two men walked away, Mr. Harris asked, "Does he always treat you so rudely?"

"Yes, unfortunately he does."

"And are you always so polite and friendly to him?"

"Yes, I am."

"Why are you so nice to him when he is so unfriendly to you?"

"Because I don't want _him_ to decide how _I'm_ going to act."

SHE STOOD ALONE

It was a crisp, cold Halloween night when Norma Hollister went out with friends to collect treats in the neighborhood. While walking from house to house, someone suggested that the group play a trick on the strange old woman who lived at the corner. Norma didn't know the woman's name—only that she was alone, had a dozen cats, and rarely ventured outside her gaudy pink house.

The shades were drawn and the house was dark. Norma joined in as the kids draped toilet paper around the yard. She hesitated when they began soaping the windows and withdrew completely when the egg-pelting started.

"What if this were happening to my grandmother?" thought Norma in anguish. She moved back into the shadows and watched as the kids continued, not knowing whether to stay or walk away. Suddenly, a light went on and the door of the house opened.

There was the old woman in a long dress, holding a cat, her white hair shining in the moonlight. As the other kids ran for cover, Norma stepped out of the shadows and just stood there, uncertain what to do. Stooped over her cane, the old woman looked extremely fragile. Norma could see that she was crying.

What were Norma's feelings? Did she act responsibly? Discuss your reactions with a classmate.

Earning, Spending, and Saving

Money. Why is it important to you? You can't eat it or wear it. You can't use it the way you use a computer, a hammer, or a spoon. Lots of people put frames around their first-earned dollars, but they do it for sentimental reasons, not because the dollars have any artistic value. What good is money anyway? Why is it so important?

The money you have in your pocket or purse right now is valuable to you because you know you can exchange it for goods—like a hamburger, a soda, a new video game, or a pair of shoes. You can also exchange your money for services—such as a bus ride, an exercise class, or a guitar lesson. Everyone will accept your money as payment—as long as you have enough of it. The same is true when you sell something (like an old bicycle or a coat you've outgrown), or provide a service for someone (such as baby-sitting or mowing a lawn). You exchange your goods and services for money, and with that money you buy the things you want or need.

If you decide to put your money in your savings account at the bank, your money performs a different function. It becomes a reserve of buying power—what bankers call a *liquid asset*. Your coat and bicycle were assets too, but you had to sell them before you could use their value to obtain anything else. A liquid asset can be spent right away. Money is the only completely liquid asset you can ever have.

Of course, you don't have to put your money in the bank. You could keep it in a mattress like the characters in old movies do.

Spending Fantasy and...

If you had enough money to buy any three things in the whole world that you wanted, what would they be?

I Would Purchase　　　**Why?**

1. _____　　_____

2. _____　　_____

3. _____　　_____

...Reality

With the amount of money you know you can really get during the next year or so, what would you like to save for? _____

Why? _____

Your Attitudes About Money

How do you get your ideas about how to earn, spend, and save money? Do you listen to what your friends say about money and copy them? Do you have your own ideas about money and tell them to your friends? Where did your ideas come from?

We often learn how to handle jobs and money from our parents and other adults around us. Sometimes adults are good models, but sometimes they have problems with money, too. Do you know an adult who is always broke and can't seem to pay his or her bills? Why does this happen? Does this person have any financial goals?

Are there adults you know who seem to be able to handle money very well? Do they have financial goals? Ask them. Find out what they do to manage their money. Maybe they can give you some ideas. You might ask the same questions of a student who handles money well.

Self-Assessment

Answer these questions:	Yes	No	Sometimes
1. I try to earn money however I can.			
2. I like to have money, but I don't like working to get it.			
3. I like money just so I can look at it and see how much I have.			
4. I like money for the things it can buy for me more than for itself.			
5. I think all the excitement about money is silly. Who needs it? Other things are more important to me.			

You may have some other feelings about money. If so, here's a place to list some of them: _____

_____

Fair Exchange?

A famous singer once gave a concert on a South Seas island. The people who lived on the island wanted to hear the singer, but they couldn't pay her in money—they didn't use money. Instead, they gave her three pigs, 23 turkeys, 44 chickens, 4,000 coconuts, and masses of bananas. **Can you imagine living in a world without money?**

Bags of Money

During times of *inflation*, there is an increase in the prices of goods and services, so the value of money goes down. Throughout history, some of the worst inflations have been caused by governments that printed a lot of extra money to help pay for wars. An amazing inflation occurred in Germany after World War I. In 1914, prior to the war, 4.2 German marks was equal to 1 dollar. After the war, in 1922, 7000 marks equaled 1 dollar. In July, 1923, 160,000 marks equaled 1 dollar; and by October 1 of the same year, 242 million marks equaled 1 dollar. One month later, in November, it took 4 billion 200 million marks to equal 1 dollar! **People had to carry their money to the store in shopping bags!**

Get a Job!

You Have Choices and...

With all the choices out there, how do people end up in the right job, career, and profession? Is it magic? ...luck? ...planning? ...hard work? Or is it a combination of things?

Does it ever seem that almost everyone you know has an idea what he or she wants out of life—everyone except you? Or do *you* know, too?

Actually, an awful lot of people really *don't* know what they want out of life. And a lot more people don't like their jobs! But *you* can avoid both of these problems.

If you start looking at the situation early enough, it's possible to find a job or career that's right for you. How? By looking first at YOU. One of the most important things to realize is that you have choices. See if you can answer the questions below:

...Possibilities

List 5 jobs or careers that you have considered for yourself or that other people have said you would be good at:

1. _____
2. _____
3. _____
4. _____
5. _____

Self-Assessment

Why do you want to work?

What are your strong points?

What are your weak points?

What are your goals?

What are your hobbies?

What lifestyle do you want?

83

Self-Assessment, cont.

Below are several groups of statements related to work. After reading each statement, write the letter of the statement above the number on the scale that best represents how true the statement is *for you*.

Recognition
A. It's important to have other people think my work is good.
B. I'd like a job that other people think highly of.
C. A job title is very important.

No ——1——2——3——4——5—— Yes

Achievement
A. When I do something, I like to do it well.
B. I want my work to lead me to better opportunities.
C. I am happiest when my work helps me learn new things.

No ——1——2——3——4——5—— Yes

Leadership.
A. I like to know that what I do causes change.
B. I enjoy planning and organizing things.
C. I enjoy showing other people how to do things.

No ——1——2——3——4——5—— Yes

Helping
A. I want my work or talents to improve the world somehow.
B. I like to help others directly.
C. I'd be happiest working in a helping organization like the Red Cross.

No ——1——2——3——4——5—— Yes

Self-expression
A. I think I'd really blossom if I found the right job or career.
B. I want to be creative at work.
C. Being able to express myself is important to me.

No ——1——2——3——4——5—— Yes

Money
A. I want to make a lot of money.
B. How much a job pays is the most important thing about it.
C. How much I make tells how successful I am.

No ——1——2——3——4——5—— Yes

Values
A. I think work builds character.
B. Having high standards is important to me.
C. I'd have a hard time working for a dishonest person.

No ——1——2——3——4——5—— Yes

Independence
A. I'd like a job or career where people depend on each other.
B. I depend primarily on myself.
C. I'd like a job that allows me to think and act on my own.

No ——1——2——3——4——5—— Yes

Creativity
A. I'd like a job or career that makes use of my originality and creative solutions.
B. I like to work with others on creative projects.
C. If there's a difficult problem, I usually want to tackle it.

No ——1——2——3——4——5—— Yes

Relationships
A. I like being part of a team of people working toward a common goal.
B. I enjoy meeting new people.
C. I like to work with people who like the things I like.

No ——1——2——3——4——5—— Yes

Interests
A. I think having the right job can make life interesting.
B. I don't like sameness; I like variety.
C. I want a job or career to be the most important thing in my life.

No ——1——2——3——4——5—— Yes

What do your answers on the self-assessment reveal about you? Write a paragraph that describes what you learned. Start by completing the sentence below. Do *not* think about a specific job or career. Concentrate on *you*.

I would like to have a job in which I can . . . _____

_____

_____

_____

_____

Compare your description to each of the five jobs you listed on the previous page.

The Way I See It...

Conflict?

You're on third base, with runners on first and second. There are two outs, the score is tied, and it's the ninth inning. The batter bunts, and you race for home. The pitcher goes after the ball and throws it to the catcher. You slide. A split second later the catcher catches the ball with one foot on the bag. You know you made it, but the umpire yells, "Out!"

Several people watch the same event and see it differently. Not only that, they react to it differently. For example, some people at the ball game agree with the umpire's call, while others think he needs to have his eyes checked. Does it mean somebody is crazy?

Probably not. The reason is more interesting.

Or Different Points of View?

It's no wonder people see the rest of the world in such different ways. There's so much going on that no two people's brains make exactly the same sense out of it. Each of us perceives the world uniquely.

When you and someone else look at an object, you don't see it exactly the same way. You might be taller, shorter, or looking at it from a different angle.

Your view of things also depends on past experiences. Often without even realizing it, you review information gained from similar events before deciding what has happened and how to react to it.

Can you think of a time recently when you reacted to something based on your past experiences? _____

_____

Are you seeing something or someone as they were and not as they are? Describe how it happened and how you mixed up the past with the present._____

_____

_____

_____

85

Do You Trust Your Perception?

Look at these drawings:

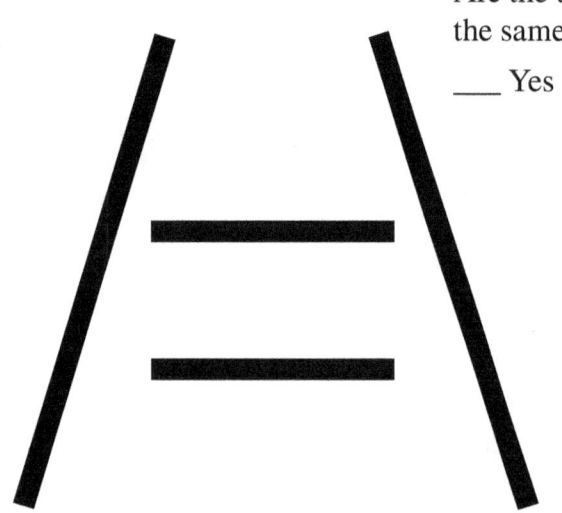

Are the two horizontal lines the same length?
___ Yes ___ No

The upper bar appears to be longer than the lower one, but they are the same length.

If you connected Line A to Line B, would they make a straight line?
___ Yes ___ No

Line AB may not look straight, but it is.

Pay Attention!

Imagine that you are watching T.V., and three commercials come on, one right after the other.
The first is for a foot powder. The second is for a clothing and shoe store. The third is for a laundry detergent. *To which would you probably give the most attention?* **Write your first thought:**

_____

Why? _____

_____

_____

_____

Unless you suffer from athlete's foot or you do the family's laundry and like it—you probably chose the clothing and shoe commercial. Your **needs and wants** influence how much attention you give to things.

The Filter of Past Experiences

People often make decisions about things that are happening in the present based partially—even wholly—on experiences from the past. For example, Joel is willing to see any movie that his favorite actor makes, regardless of what the critics or other people say about it. Dianne, who got sick a couple of hours after eating Sushi for the very first time, absolutely refuses to try it again and gets queasy at the sight of it.

Rachel, who did well in Math in elementary school, is confident that she can master Trigonometry, while Marty, who did poorly on his first Trig test, is equally certain that he will fail.

Have you ever had trouble clearly seeing someone in the present because of how you felt about that person in the past? When people change, isn't it only fair that our perceptions change, too?

Describe how you recently reacted to something or someone based on your past experiences:

_____

_____

_____

_____

To Trust or Not to Trust

Whom Do You Trust?

...and Why?

What does it mean to trust someone? The dictionary says that *to trust* means "to place confidence in" or "to rely on for truthfulness or accuracy." A famous writer, G.K. Chesterton, wrote these lines:

We are all in the same boat in a stormy sea, and we owe each other a terrible loyalty.

Loyalty, confidence, reliability, belief in. All of these words have something to do with trust.

On the lines below, write the names of five people whom you trust:

1. _____
2. _____
3. _____
4. _____
5. _____

Now pick one of these people and explain why you trust him or her: _____
_____
_____
_____
_____

Do you trust this person enough to talk to him or her about things that are personal and private to you? _____
_____

Can you think of a time when it was very hard or impossible for you to trust someone? What were your reasons? _____
_____
_____
_____
_____
_____
_____

Which of these qualities do you look for when deciding whether to trust a person? Add any other qualities you can think of and number the qualities from most important (1) to least important (12 or...):

___ willing to listen
___ accepting
___ sensitive
___ honest
___ energetic
___ loving
___ understanding
___ aware
___ helpful
___ responsive
___ experienced
___ reliable
___ intelligent
___ well known to you
___ _____
___ _____
___ _____

Look again at the list of people you trust. How do they measure up to these qualities?

Who Trusts You?

Make a list of some people who trust *you*:

1. _____
2. _____
3. _____
4. _____
5. _____
6. _____

Pick one person and tell why you believe he or she trusts you. Write the reasons here:

_____
_____
_____
_____
_____

Here are some ways you can show that you are trustworthy:

- Consider how your behavior will affect the feelings and lives of others.

- Have as much concern for the feelings of others as you have for your own feelings.

- Try to drop your defenses and false fronts.

- Accept others as they are.

- Change your negative attitudes and behaviors toward other people.

- Understand and respect yourself.

- Follow through. Always do what you say you are going to do.

- Tell the truth.

Who Doesn't?

Describe a time when it was important to you to be trusted by someone who wouldn't trust you:

_____
_____
_____
_____
_____
_____
_____
_____
_____
_____
_____
_____
_____
_____

Try These Exercises

1 The Noggin Lifter. Do this exercise with a partner. Have your partner lie on the floor. Explain that he or she should relax as much as possible and trust you. Then, take your partner's head in both hands and lift it off the floor. Gently rotate your partner's head from side to side. See if you can make it seem separate from his or her body. You may find that at first your partner has a hard time relaxing and giving up control. But the more your partner trusts you, the easier the exercise becomes. After a few minutes, trade places with your partner and have him or her lift and rotate your "noggin."

2 The Trust Walk. This exercise is also done with a partner *in silence*. Blindfold your partner and take him or her for a walk. Put one hand around your partner's waist and gently but firmly hold his or her elbow or forearm with your other hand. Guide your partner to touch, smell, and hear many different things. Make the experience adventurous but safe. After about 15 minutes, reverse roles. Afterwards, discuss with your partner the trust—or lack of it—that each of you experienced, and why.

Helping

Help can be good to give and get. It can lift the weight off someone's back—or mind. Helping another person can be a generous thing to do. It can be brave and unselfish, and is often instructive. Helping can cause the person who receives the help to feel grateful and the person who gives the help to feel rewarded. Helping can build friendships.

Sometimes help is given or received for the wrong reasons. Help is sometimes used as a way to gain power over another person. It can be used to insult someone or to interfere with his or her life. Unwelcome help can make a person feel resentful. Help that is forced on someone can make the person feel like a victim.

A Story About Help

Debbie and Shirley are friends. They are in the ninth grade. One day when Shirley was over at Debbie's house, they went into the tool shed to get something and there was Butch, Debbie's little brother. Butch was trying to saw a piece of wood in two.

Debbie and Shirley watched Butch for a moment. He was working hard, but having trouble. Debbie knew that she could saw the piece of wood much faster and better than Butch.

"Want some help, Butch?" she asked.

"No, thanks," grunted Butch. "This is tough, but I can do it."

"Okay," replied Debbie. She turned to Shirley and said, "Come on. Let's go."

After they left the shed, Shirley turned to Debbie and said, "Butch sure was having a hard time. Don't you think you or I should have done that for him?"

"No," answered Debbie.

"Why not?" asked Shirley. "It was clear that he needed help."

"Yeah, it was a struggle for him, but there are some things you have to struggle with if you're going to learn how to do them," responded Debbie. "Besides, Butch said he wanted to do it himself."

"Hmmm," said Shirley as she thought about what Debbie said. "Yeah, that's right," she added. "I remember how I felt last Saturday. I was trying to make tacos and my big brother kept getting in my way. He said he was helping but he was really trying to take over. I got so frustrated that I started yelling. Then he yelled back. It was awful. He's good at making tacos, but I've got to have a chance to learn how to do it my own way."

"Right," answered Debbie.

Take a few minutes to answer the questions on the next page.

How to Help

When you see someone who appears to need help, unless it is an obvious emergency, don't just jump in. First, find out if the person wants help. There's an important difference between needing help and wanting help.

Recall some of your own experiences. Think of a time when you had a task to complete or a problem to solve, and you didn't feel like doing it alone. You *wanted* help, but you didn't really *need* help. You were perfectly capable of completing the job or solving the problem on your own.

Another time you may have *needed* help because you didn't know how to do something. But you didn't *want* the help. Maybe you liked the challenge of having to figure it out alone, or were too proud to accept help.

How can you find out whether someone needs and/or wants help? One way is to ask. Another way is to quietly look at the situation and figure it out for yourself. Then if you feel that your help will be truly appreciated, offer it to the person. He or she can do one of two things—refuse the help or take it. It's that simple! *But in offering help, be sure you're ready to accept either answer.*

Questions

Have you ever insisted on helping someone even though the person resisted your help? Describe what happened and how you and the other person felt about the situation and each other.

_____
_____
_____
_____
_____
_____
_____

Describe a time when *you* were forced to accept help that you didn't want. *How did you feel about your "helper?" What did you do?*

_____
_____
_____
_____
_____
_____
_____

Things to Try

1 **Notice how people ask for help.** Do they ask for it kindly, or do they seem to expect it? Do they ask directly, or do they beat around the bush and hint at their need for help? Do they seem to have to overcome fear or pride to ask for help? Can they ask for help freely, or do they seem to be embarrassed?

2 **Examine your own life for examples of times when you needed *and* wanted help.** By looking at these examples, you can become a better helper. So take a look inward and see what you can discover about yourself and helping. *When do you want help? When does someone else's "help" get in your way? How do you let people know you want help? What do you do after you receive help? What do you do before you help someone? Do you expect anything in return from the people you help? What?*

3 **Talk to a professional helper.** For example, a social worker, counselor, or psychologist. Ask for that person's views on helping. For example: *What skills would better equip you to assist others when they ask for your help? Where can people go for professional help? In what situations should you try to get professional help for a friend, whether the friend asks for it or not? How should you go about it?*

Managing Conflict

Good Conflicts...   ...and Bad

Everybody gets involved in an argument or fight now and then. Conflict is normal.

Think back to conflicts you've gotten into. Some may have been necessary, maybe even helpful. Others were probably terrible events that you hate to think about now. *What makes you feel good about some conflicts and bad about others?*

"Good" conflicts allow people to deal with things that are bothering them. They clear the air and give everyone a new start. After these kinds of conflicts are over, people usually end up feeling okay. "Bad" conflicts may also clear the air. But they usually leave people feeling bad about the other person, themselves, and the relationship.

Good Conflicts...

Think of a time when you got into a conflict and it turned out well. *How did the conflict start?*

_____
_____
_____

What did your opponent in the conflict want? _____

_____
_____

What did you want?

_____
_____
_____

How was the conflict resolved?

_____
_____
_____

...and Bad

Think of a time when you were involved in a conflict and it turned out poorly. *How did the conflict start?*

_____
_____
_____

What did your opponent want? _____

_____
_____

What did you want?

_____
_____
_____

What was the result?

_____
_____
_____

Three Kinds of Conflict

1. LOSE-LOSE

What Happens:
- Physical or verbal violence on the part of both parties.

Results:
- Bodies and/or feelings get hurt.
- Things are worse than they were at first.
- Both people disrespect each other.
- Both people disrespect themselves.

2. WIN-LOSE

What Happens:
- One person uses physical or verbal violence.
- The other person gives in or runs away.

Results:
- One person gets hurt and the other gets his or her way.
- Both people disrespect each other.
- Both people disrespect themselves.

3. WIN-WIN

What Happens:
- No one attacks anyone else in a physical or verbal way.
- Each person states his or her feelings and thoughts about the disagreement.
- Each person lets the other know that he or she is listening.
- Suggestions for settling the disagreement are offered and one is mutually agreed upon.

Results:
- No one is badly hurt.
- The disagreement is settled, often through compromise.
- Both people respect each other.
- Both people respect themselves.

When you are in a conflict (or about to be in one), there are several things that you can do to help the conflict follow the WIN-WIN course shown on the chart. These things are called *strategies*. Conflict management strategies are discussed in a separate activity sheet. For now, let's look at three fairly common responses to conflict that usually *make things worse*.

Violence. Physical violence (hurting someone's body) or verbal violence (hurting someone's feelings) destroys relationships and rarely deals with the real problem. If someone is about to murder you, then you may have to be violent in return to protect yourself. But 99 percent of the time, physical or verbal violence is not the answer.

Flight. You can physically run or hide from a conflict, or you can "cop out" by failing to stand up for yourself. Either way, you lose both self-respect and the respect of your opponent. And while you are hiding, the conflict is still there, so nothing gets resolved.

Telling. Also known as squealing or tattling, telling usually just makes your opponent madder and the conflict worse. Telling on your opponent is not the same as asking for help. When you ask for help, you are looking for a solution. When you tell on your opponent, you are trying to get him or her in trouble. **Note:** *Always* go for help if you think you are in danger.

How to Resolve a Conflict

Have you ever been in a conflict? **Of course!** No matter how much you may try to avoid them, conflicts happen. They are part of life. What makes conflicts upsetting or scary is not knowing how to handle them. If you don't know something constructive to do when strong emotions start churning inside, the results can be, well, explosive! So study these strategies and next time you see a conflict looming, take a deep breath and...

Try a Conflict-Management Strategy

Listen—Actively!

Often people get into conflicts because they don't really listen to each other or they misunderstand what they hear. So try really listening to the other person's point of view. Tune in to the words—and the feelings, too. To let the person know that you are listening, say things like:

"Okay, I'm listening."

"Let me see if I heard you right. You said... ."

"Go ahead. You talk first and I'll listen."

Use "I" Messages

Show the other person that you are willing to take responsibility for your feelings and the way you view the conflict. Don't use name-calling, blaming "you" messages. For example, don't say:

"Hey stupid, you busted into line. Get back where you belong!"

Instead, say what you think and how you feel, with an "I" message, like:

"I was next in line. I feel cheated when someone cuts in after I've been waiting so long."

Abandon the Scene

To leave the scene may sound like running away, but it's different. Abandoning is realizing that nothing but harm can happen if you try to say or do anything at the time. Sometimes it's best to just leave things alone. For instance, suppose you are walking down the street and a group of gang members runs you off the sidewalk. You'd probably only make matters worse if you tried to work things out with them.

Conflict-Management Strategies, cont.

Take Turns

Some conflicts happen because two people want the same thing at the same time. Show the other person that you are willing to be second sometimes. Do things like flip a coin, draw straws, guess a number between one and ten, or say, "You go first because you're older."

Get Assistance

Bring someone into the conflict who can help settle it. This may sound like telling, but it's not. Telling is trying to get the other person in trouble; getting assistance is asking another person to help straighten things out. For example, if you and a friend disagree about the requirements on an assignment, ask your teacher.

Try to Compromise

If you are willing to give up *a little* of what you want, and the other person is too, then you can both have at least *part* of what you want. That's a compromise. You compromise when you make suggestions like these:

"I'll take half and you take half."

"I'll go to the park with you in the morning, if you'll go to the mall with me in the afternoon."

"I'll mow the lawn and you sweep the walk."

Express Regret

Let the other person know that you are sorry the conflict happened. You don't have to admit you are wrong or that the conflict is your fault. Just say something like this:

"It's too bad this happened."
or
"I know you're upset and I feel bad about it."

Postpone Action

If you are mad, tired, hungry, or in a hurry—or if you think the other person is—wait. Put off dealing with the conflict until later. Say:

"Everything seems to be going wrong. I'm too tired to think straight. Could we get back to this later?"
or
"I want to settle this, but now's not the time. What about waiting until after lunch?"

Problem-Solve

This method requires that both (or all) parties in the conflict be willing to search for a "win-win" solution. Here are the steps involved:

1. Define the conflict in terms of each person's needs, not competing solutions. Remember to use "I" messages and active listening.

2. Together, brainstorm possible alternatives and then evaluate them.

3. Pick the alternative that has the best chance of meeting the needs of both (or all) parties in the conflict.

4. Together, implement the solution.

5. Get back together later, and discuss how well the solution worked.

Work with Yourself

- **Discover what your conflict "buttons" are.** These are sore spots that cause you to lose your temper. Evaluate them, to see if they're reasonable or not. Naturally, there are times when you have a right to be angry.

Notice your behavior when your buttons are pushed. Is it easy for you to think or do things when your emotions take over? Knowing these things will help you stay in control and use conflict-management strategies.

- **Make yourself an all-purpose target.** It helps to have something to take out your anger on so that you don't hurt anyone. Your target can be a pillow, a punching bag, a doll, a dartboard, and so on. For many people, a sport like handball, aerobics, running, or swimming does the trick.

What Is Justice?

According to Webster...

How many times have you had thoughts like these:
"That isn't fair!"
"It serves him right!"
"He did what was right."
"She got what she deserved."
"I'd do the same thing if I were him."
"I won't do that because it would be wrong."

You have a sense of justice. You've been developing it for years. Maybe you call it *fairness*. The dictionary says that justice is:

The quality of being just, impartial, or fair; the principle or ideal of just dealing or right action; conformity to a principle or ideal.

...and You

Judges and attorneys make decisions about justice every day. But so do businesspeople, teachers, parents, and elected officials. We all do! **How do you define justice?** Read the items on the next page and decide whether each one is just or unjust. Be sure to explain your reasons. Then get together with one or two classmates and compare and discuss your answers.

Special Brands of Justice

Write a creative paragraph to illustrate each of the following terms.

Frontier justice: _____

Poetic justice: _____

"Eye-for-an-eye" justice: _____

Evenhanded justice: _____

You Decide: Just or Unjust?

1. A woman spanks her child in the supermarket because he keeps doing things that get on her nerves.
____Just ____Unjust
Your reason: _____
_____
_____

2. A man who enjoys nude sunbathing tells his neighbors he is not going to stop just because it bothers them.
____Just ____Unjust
Your reason: _____
_____
_____

3. Half of the people working for a U.S. senator in his Washington office are members of his family.
____Just ____Unjust
Your reason: _____
_____
_____

4. In a waiting room where no one is smoking, someone lights up a cigarette.
____Just ____Unjust
Your reason: _____
_____
_____

5. A judge dismisses the case against a woman caught shoplifting because the police forgot to read her rights when she was arrested.
____Just ____Unjust
Your reason: _____
_____
_____

6. A woman charged with first-degree murder pleads guilty to second-degree murder and receives a sentence of 15 years to life in prison.
____Just ____Unjust
Your reason: _____
_____
_____

7. A man who pleads innocent to first-degree murder, but is convicted, receives the death penalty.
____Just ____Unjust
Your reason: _____
_____
_____

8. Without the consent of Congress, the President of the United States commits the military to defend a foreign nation against an aggressor.
____Just ____Unjust
Your reason: _____
_____
_____

9. A police officer sees a man snatch a woman's purse. The officer yells, "Halt," but the man keeps running. The officer fires a warning shot, but the man continues to run. The officer shoots the man dead.
____Just ____Unjust
Your reason: _____
_____
_____

10. A prominent banker charged with cheating investors out of millions of dollars by selling them worthless bonds pleads guilty to a lesser charge and is sentenced to one-thousand hours of community service and three years probation.
____Just ____Unjust
Your reason: _____
_____
_____

11. A drunk driver kills a 17-year-old bicyclist, pleads guilty, and is released from prison on probation after serving 18 months.
____Just ____Unjust
Your reason: _____
_____
_____

Tales of Justice

The Driscoll's Fruit

You and some of your friends are hungry. You're walking through the alley together when one of your friends notices that the fruit on the trees in the Driscoll's back yard is ripe and looking good. All your friends start climbing the fence and calling to you, "Come on. The car isn't in the driveway. The Driscoll's probably aren't home."

You know both Driscolls drive, which means that one of them might be home. Mr. Driscoll has a terrible temper. You also remember all the times you helped the Driscolls with their yard work. Mr. Driscoll promised to pay you and give you some of the fruit, and he hasn't done either yet. Your mother wouldn't let you ask the Driscolls for the money several days after you had done the work. So you were never quite sure whether they simply weren't going to pay you or they had forgotten.

What Would You Do?

Read each of the following reactions. Put a check (√) beside the one that describes what you would *most likely* do. Put an (X) beside any that reflect what you *might* do.

A.____ You don't go for the fruit because it would be stealing, and stealing is against the law.

B.____ You ask your friends not to take the fruit because you believe it would be stealing. Then you go to the Driscolls' front door to remind them that they owe you the money and the fruit.

C.____ You go for the fruit with your friends because you just can't wait to taste it.

D.____ You don't join your friends because you're afraid of Mr. Driscoll's temper.

E.____ You go for the fruit because your friends are doing it.

F.____ You ask your friends not to take the fruit because you know you wouldn't like it if someone came on your property and took something of yours. Then you go to the Driscoll's front door and ask them if you can pick up the fruit they owe you.

G.____ You go for the fruit because you believe the Driscolls owe it to you.

H.____ You don't join your friends because you think you might get caught and are afraid of the consequences.

...and Not Do?

Is there a difference between what you'd *like* to do and what you probably *would* do? Explain:

_____
_____
_____
_____
_____

Compare your choices with those of one or two classmates. Discuss how your thinking is similar and different. Follow the same process with the story on the next page.

The Hundred-Dollar Dilemma

You have a dog that was given to you by one of your best friends. You haven't treated the dog as well as you know you should have, and at times your brother and sister have gotten upset with you about it. Suddenly your dog becomes very sick, and you know inside that it's because of the way you've neglected it.

You call the vet and describe the symptoms. She responds that it sounds pretty hopeless, but she is willing to try to save the dog. She explains that you will need to bring the dog to her immediately. You will also be required to make a one-hundred dollar deposit. The vet does not extend credit, and she is the only one in town.

You and your brother and sister have been saving to buy a new home-entertainment system for your parents' 25th wedding anniversary. The money is in the bank. You've put in over a hundred dollars, and now you want it for your dog, but your brother and sister say no. They are sure your dog is going to die, and they know that without your money, they'll never be able to buy the home-entertainment system in time for the anniversary. They tell you they're sorry about your dog, but they're not going to let you ruin the surprise for your parents just because you feel guilty. They suggest that you take the dog to the animal shelter and have him put to sleep.

Later, after your brother and sister have left the house, you are alone with a couple of your friends. They agree with you that an effort should be made to save the dog, regardless of whether he lives or dies. You know that your brother has just cashed his paycheck and that his money (over a hundred dollars) is in his top drawer. And you know where the key is.

What Would You Do?

A. ____ You don't take the money because it's against the law to steal. You take your dog to the shelter and have him put to sleep because it's the "right" thing to do.

B. ____ You take the money, and you take your dog to the vet because you don't want to feel guilty anymore.

C. ____ You think about who will be hurt the most by your actions. You decide that because your dog is suffering so much and still has a chance to live, it's best to face all the trouble you'll experience with your family, so you take the money.

D. ____ You tell your friends you're going to take the dog to the vet because you want them to think you're a good person. Then after they leave, you take him to the animal shelter and have him put to sleep.

E. ____ You take the money, and you take the dog to the vet. You don't think that laws against stealing apply in this case. You reason that your brother and sister have a hundred dollars of money that you earned, and that you have an obligation to take care of your dog. You plan to tell your brother what you did right away and to pay him back with the hundred dollars in the bank.

F. ____ You don't take the money because if you did, you would be stealing something that didn't belong to you, and because you agreed to cooperate with your brother and sister to buy the home-entertainment system. You take the dog to the animal shelter and have him put to sleep because you are concerned about the pain he is in.

G. ____ You don't touch your brother's money because you're afraid of how you would be punished. Your dog dies.

H. ____ You think about who will be hurt the most by your actions. You decide, since the animal is suffering so much, to put him out of his misery right away. You feel that the joy your parents will experience when they find out that their children have saved enough money to buy them a nice gift is of higher value than attempting to prolong the life of a very sick animal.

Showing Initiative

What Does It Mean?

Initiative means the ability to begin, or to follow through, with a plan or task. It also means taking the first step even if you're the one to make the opening move. It can mean finding and doing things that need to be done without being told to do them. Finding things that need to be done takes alertness and creativity. Doing them takes determination. For these reasons, people who show initiative are highly valued by there teachers, and employers, and others around them. People who show initiative are the ones who tend to get ahead in life!

One of the most obvious ways you can take initiative is by doing things that involve skills and talents you already possess. Think about what you like to do and what you're good at doing. Once you know what your especially good at train yourself to spot tasks that require that skill. Then do these tasks, or volunteer to do them.

My Skills and Talents

What are you good at?

1. What do I do especially well?

_____
_____
_____
_____

2. What can I do quickly and efficiently?

_____
_____
_____
_____

3. What tasks do I enjoy most at home?

_____
_____

At school?

_____
_____

On a team?

_____
_____

In a club?

_____
_____

DO IT NOW!

Nothing impresses as much as immediate follow up. If you say you'll do something that needs to be done, take action right away. Don't waver, falter, vacillate, or procrastinate. When you put things off, they just get worse and more difficult to accomplish. Do it Now!

1. Describe a time when you did a chore or a task without being told.

   _____
   _____
   _____

2. What made you decide to do it?

   _____
   _____
   _____

3. How did other people react?

   _____
   _____
   _____

4. When was the last time you offered someone a helpful suggestion?

   _____

   What was it and how did it occur?

   _____
   _____
   _____

It's My Job

Have you ever said (or heard someone say), "That's not my job" when faced with a disagreeable or difficult task? Have you ever responded, "It's good enough the way it is" when asked to redo something? The enemy of initiative is being satisfied with mediocre work or "getting by" under current conditions no matter how bad they are. If you tend to have attitudes like these, work to change them. Strive instead to take responsibility for making things better. Pay attention to the different areas of your life: home, school, jobs, clubs, sports teams, etc. What needs to be done that you could do?

List some of your ideas below.

_____   _____
_____   _____
_____   _____
_____   _____

What's stopping you from doing these things? Take the initiative and JUST DO IT!

If your heart is in Social-Emotional Learning, visit us online.

Come see us at
www.InnerchoicePublishing.com

Our web site gives you a look at all our other Social-Emotional Learning-based books, free activities, articles, research, and learning and teaching strategies. Every week you'll get a new Sharing Circle topic and lesson.

INNERCHOICE Publishing
15079 Oak Chase Court
Wellington, FL 33414

www.ingramcontent.com/pod-product-compliance
Lightning Source LLC
Chambersburg PA
CBHW081925170426
43200CB00014B/2837